To Serena,

Dario Fo

7/11/07

OVER MY DEAD BODY

Some Grave Questions for God

David J. Forman

gefen
publishing house
JERUSALEM ◆ NEW YORK

Typesetting: Marzel A.S. – Jerusalem

Cover Design: Studio Paz, Jerusalem

Adapted from the stained glass window above the ark in the main sanctuary of
Congregation B'nai Israel of Boca Raton, Florida. It conveys God's presence at all
times. The artist is Mr. William Buchanan of Boca Raton, who worked from a
concept by Rabbi Richard Agler.

ISBN 965-229-351-2

3 5 7 9 8 6 4 2

Gefen Publishing House
6 Hatzvi Street, Jerusalem 94386, Israel
972-2-538-0247
orders@gefenpublishing.com

Gefen Books
600 Broadway, Lynbrook, NY 11563, USA
516-593-1234
orders@gefenpublishing.com

www.israelbooks.com

Printed in Israel   *Send for our free catalogue*

There are places I'll remember
All my life, though some have changed.
Some forever, not for better,
Some have gone and some remain.
All these places have their moments —
With lovers and friends I still can recall.
Some are dead and some are living.
In my life, I've loved them all.

(*In My Life* by The Beatles)

For Myron Kinberg
Leslie Brenner
Karen Smith Senyak

"The memory of the righteous is a blessing"

(Proverbs 10:7)

For Dorritt Forman

"The world exists only because of
the innocent breath of children"

(Talmud Shabbat 119b)

For Phyllis Forman

"It is not the home that gives honor to a human being,
But the human being who gives honor to the home"

(Talmud Ta'anit 21b)

❖ ❖ ❖

For Lucille Bayes Hamburger

"Wisdom is an attribute of age"

(Job 12:12)

Also by David J. Forman

Israel on Broadway, America: Off-Broadway — Jews in the New Millennium

Jewish Schizophrenia in the Land of Israel

Fifty Ways to be Jewish, or: Simon & Garfunkel, Jesus Loves You <u>Less</u> than You Will Know

Praise for
Israel on Broadway, America: Off-Broadway –
Jews in the New Millennium

In *Israel on Broadway*, David Forman presents a bold and controversial approach to issues of Jewish identity. He challenges Diaspora Jews to actively engage Israel. Not everyone will agree with his views, but anyone who cares about the continued vitality of Israel and the perpetuity of the Jewish people must read this book.

Alan Dershowitz, Professor, Harvard Law School, Author of The Case for Israel

David Forman has presented a comprehensive, incisive and honest analysis of the relationship between Israel and Diaspora Jewry. This is obligatory reading.

A.B. Yehoshua, Israeli Author

In this strongly and persuasively argued book, Rabbi David Forman presents a powerful plea for health: the health and survival of the Jewish people.

Sir Martin Gilbert, Author of The Israelis

Bold, cutting to the quick, *Israel on Broadway* provoked me. When it was wrong it drove me crazy, when it was right, it made holes in my heart. I could spend the next ten years arguing with these pages.

Anne Roiphe, Author of Lovingkindness

David Forman is my kind of rabbi — smart, witty, insightful and reverently irreverent. Few know more than he does about Israel-Diaspora relations. Read this book. You'll enjoy it and learn something.

Ze'ev Chafets, New York Daily News

This is a passionate Zionist polemic, which juxtaposes the situation of Jews in Israel and the United States. This provocative book will stimulate debate among American Jews about the nature of their Jewish identity and commitment.

Dr. Paula Hyman, Lucy Moses Professor of Modern Jewish History, Yale University

Israel on Broadway is the book that Lenny Bruce would have written had he been in search of a healthy Jewish identity. For Forman, the challenge of the contemporary Jew is to learn the Jewish drama — to claim it, to participate in it and to write the next great act.

Dr. Bernard Steinberg, Director, Harvard Hillel, Harvard University

Praise for *Jewish Schizophrenia in the Land of Israel*

David Forman offers us a painful analysis of the spirit of today's Israel, along with fresh observations on how we have gotten into our collective malaise, and how to recover. His insights are fierce, poignant and original.

Amos Oz, *Israeli Author*

With wit and charm, David Forman helps readers navigate the psychological landscape of modern Israel. Whether writing about house demolitions or sexual antics of political leaders or the existential meaning of Jerusalem to the Jewish people, he helps Israel find its true self. Forman puts Israel "on the couch," offering some healing to the patient with both spiritual insight and a hearty laugh.

Charles M. Sennott, *Boston Globe*

With a keen eye and razor-sharp wit, and with an uncanny ability to cut to the heart of the matter, David Forman paints a picture of Israel that is both painful and heart-warming. Insightful and spellbinding, each page embraces a hope for a better future for the people of Israel.

Avraham Burg, *Former Speaker of the Israeli Knesset*

Praise for *Fifty Ways to be Jewish, or: Simon & Garfunkel, Jesus Loves You <u>Less</u> than You Will Know*

One need be neither a Jew nor a member of the Simon & Garfunkel generation to endorse wholeheartedly Rabbi Forman's thesis — that, at its best, religion envelops the entire world.

Professor Huston Smith, *Author of The World's Religions*

David Forman is a child of the Sixties who has refused to give up his idealism and his insistence that our world can be made better through our collective efforts. He is a "sweet survivor." Bravo for *50 Ways to be Jewish*.

Peter Yarrow *(Peter, Paul and Mary)*

50 Ways to be Jewish is a personal, eclectic, traditional but innovative guide to Judaism for those who do not know the "hows" and "whys" of Jewish living. Forman's "Ways" range from the predictable (synagogue, Sabbath, Jewish holidays) to the edgy (sex life, gay and lesbians) to the intriguing ("Your Sports" and "Your Sinatra"). As Forman writes, Jewishness is living with "care, sensitivity, thoroughness, respect, dignity, reflection and wisdom."

Steve Lipman, *Jewish Week*

CONTENTS

Acknowledgments

Over My Dead Body: Some Grave Questions for God, is a companion piece to my previous work, *50 Ways to Be Jewish*. As with *50 Ways to be Jewish*, I turned to friends and family, inviting them to think of questions about God that they have often asked themselves. Very soon I had accumulated over one hundred questions. Paring them down to the present thirty-six was not an easy task; but again, with help from those same friends and family, I was able to give expression to those primary concerns about God that seemed to occupy them and me. I shall be ever in their debt (particularly rabbis Joshua Haberman, Mayer Perelmuter, Haim Skirball and David Wilfond) for guiding me through the exhaustive process of questioning such an elusive figure as God.

Unlike my other literary ventures, this one did not intrude upon family time. Now being retired, I was able to organize my work in a way that would not deprive us of the time to be together that we so cherish. As always, they encouraged me throughout my labors.

I also wish to express my gratitude to my editors, Ms. Esther Herskovics and Ms. Laura Singer, who not only provided stylistic improvements, but also valuable insights that helped to lend greater clarity to my thoughts. I am especially grateful to all those at Gefen Publishing House. Their blend of personal and professional support accords a writer an environment that nurtures his or her creative energies.

Because of its subject matter, I wish to dedicate this book to some exceptional people — departed and living:

Myron Kinberg, a rabbinic colleague whose gentle warmth embraced all those who had the honor to know him and be touched by him; **Leslie Brenner**, a friend who always made everyone feel as if he or she were the center of attention, and who, throughout her illness in her latter years, only knew how to encourage those who were in her presence; **Karen Smith Senyak**, a classmate from a nostalgic period in my life, whose quiet demeanor, yet resolute strength, evokes only the fondest memories. All three were touched by Divinity, and, sadly, were taken from us in our hour of need, well before their hour of ultimate fulfillment.

Dorritt Forman, the sister I never knew, who died at the age of twelve in a trolley-car accident five years before my birth. How painfully her death affected my parents I will never fully grasp. To honor my parents who are no longer here to keep her memory alive, I choose to acknowledge the brief moments of joy she gave them.

Phyllis Forman, my sister-in-law, who showed us how to face death in the same way that she lived life — with dignity.

❖ ❖ ❖

Lucille Bayes Hamburger, my aunt. May she, the last of my parents' generation, continue to live a long life; and may I, in growing older, be as accepting of life's wonders and tragedies as she is.

April, 2005

Fear

There are moments in my life when I am so filled with contentment, when my love for my family is so overflowing, that I can't imagine ever letting go. I want life to stand still, knowing, of course, that such a wish will never be granted. When all is right with one's world, there is a desperate need to hold on, not to relinquish happiness. And so, sometimes at night, lying in bed, I am suddenly overcome with total panic, so overwhelming that I think I will literally fall to pieces, and cry out: "I don't want to die — I am afraid of dying." I physically cling to my wife for "dear life," to find refuge from this tidal wave of absolute horror.

My greatest fear concerning death is that I will no longer be able to tell my wife and children and grandchildren how much I love them. But, even more painful: I'll never again hear those words from their lips. They are the witnesses to my life, testifying to my worth as a human being, and I to theirs. When thoughts such as these overtake me, I can feel the other side of my heartbeat fading.

Little can calm my bouts of dread of my approaching death. Recovery and eventual sleep result from the emotional and physical exhaustion that I expend on my not so irrational fright. Often I think that I should seek professional help in dealing with this phenomenon, but, just the thought of discussing my own demise is enough to send me off into a flight of hysteria. Such is the case when I read books about death, like Maurice Lamm's *The Jewish Way in Death and Mourning*, Leon Wieseltier's *Kaddish*, Earl Grollman's many writings dealing with issues of death as they relate to surviving family members, and the ground-breaking work by Elisabeth Kübler-Ross, *On Death and Dying*. And yet, I attend funerals, even conduct them in my role as a rabbi, and am perfectly accepting — cool and collected, but not emotionally detached. I can deal with other people's deaths, as painful as their loss may be, but not with my own.

It is odd that I rarely think of sudden death, but only of my eventual passing due to natural causes. I also do not consider that I may endure infirmities, both mental and physical, that so often evolve in the course of the natural process of aging, even though my mother suffered from dementia and my father from heart disease. After all, they both lived into their nineties. When I see friends unexpectedly struck dead by a heart attack or succumb to cancer, for some odd reason (despite my own two brushes with death — one in war and one as a result of a routine liver biopsy gone wrong), as fragile as I know life to be, I do not envision such things happening to me. To me, old age is always a few years older than I am.

Holocaust survivor and Nobel Peace Prize-winning author, Elie Wiesel, tells the Hasidic[1] tale of a nineteenth century tourist from the United States who visited a famous Polish rabbi, the Hafetz Hayim. He was astonished to see that the rabbi's home was only a simple room filled with books. The only furniture was a table and a bench.

> **Tourist**: Rabbi, where is your furniture?
> **Rabbi**: Where is yours?
> **Tourist**: Mine? But I'm only a visitor here.
> **Rabbi**: So am I.

This is what I find so frightening, that we are all guests of existence. When we die, everyone else's story goes on, but we are not there to

---

1. A religious movement established in the eighteenth century by the Baal Shem Tov (see page 58), Hasidism teaches that zeal, prayer with emotional feeling and humility are superior to study.

discover how it turns out. Our lives stop in the middle. They do not reach a conclusion, they simply stop. The middle of the story is where all our stories end. We no longer play an active role in the lives of our families. Perhaps it is such thoughts that drive me crazy. How will my children survive my death? What will happen to them? Yet, "if a messenger were to come to us with the offer that death should be overthrown, but with one inseparable condition that birth should also cease; if the existing generation were given the chance to live forever, but on the clear understanding that never again would there be a child, a youth, or first love, never again new persons with new hopes, new ideas, new achievements; ourselves for always and never any others — could the answer be in doubt" (excerpted from the *Gates of Repentance* — Memorial Service — Central Conference of American Rabbis' prayer book)?

On the other hand, we can be in denial, so enraptured by our own existence that the thought of our death is unreal. After all, when we are alive, it is extremely difficult to imagine things happening without our being present to experience them. While this may seem a typical example of youthful exuberance, it also afflicts those of us older souls who are overwhelmed with the wonder of ourselves. But, not me. I know that American playwright Arthur Miller's words are true: "Immortality is like trying to carve your initials in a block of ice in the middle of July"!

I know I have been granted the gift of life although I did nothing to deserve it. I know I should be grateful for the allotted time granted me, and thus must use that time-span between birth (over which I had no control) and death (about which I have no choice), and use it wisely. Time waits for no one. It could be said that God created time so that everything would not happen at once. Indeed, if we lived forever, we could constantly postpone everything. However, given the finitude of time, we cannot. As we accept life, so too must we accept mortality as part of the bargain. And so, death becomes as much a part of life as birth; and we live in the interval between two eternities. We are obliged to render something of meaning out of that finite piece of eternity.

This all sounds good — sane — reasonable. So, why am I so petrified? The most frightening element of death is waiting for it, knowing that it is inevitable. I still wake up in the middle of the night in a pool of sweat, not at all comforted by the thought that others may feel as I do, that it is only natural to react this way to the "great unknown." I admit it: I am selfish. And, I don't understand it. Why did God create human beings only to let them die? While I cannot fathom what an alternative course might be, I would think that God could have conceived of one.

❖ ❖ ❖

Hence, this book of Divine questions — thirty-six in all. Why thirty-six? Jewish legend speaks of the *lamed-vavnikim* (Hebrew for "thirty-six righteous individuals") who toil unnoticed in their work for *tikkun olam* (Hebrew for "repairing the world"). These thirty-six righteous people roam the world in each generation. They perform acts of kindness, taking pity on the poor and showing compassion to the helpless, and leave as quietly as they arrive with only their good deeds attesting to their one-time presence. Tradition tells us that on the merit of these thirty-six people, God sustains the world from generation to generation. The concept, though adopted by Hasidism, has its roots in the *Talmud*,[1] which testifies that in every generation, thirty-six righteous people greet the Divine Presence (*Sanhedrin* 97b; *Sukkah* 45b).

---

1. The comprehensive designation for the *Mishnah* and the *Gemara* as a single unit (see page 117, footnote 1). There are two *Talmuds* — Babylonian and Jerusalem. The *Jerusalem Talmud* contains a commentary on thirty-nine of sixty-three tractates of the *Mishnah*, developed in academies in ancient Israel. Its editing was completed in the fourth century. The *Babylonian Talmud*, generally considered the more precise (and most widely used), was set down in Babylonian centers of learning between the third and fifth centuries, and covers thirty-seven tractates of the *Mishnah*.

For me, the only way to conquer my fear of dying was to write this book. Even though this is a fictionalized account of my imminent demise, the very fact that I was able to conjure up such a narrative is a step in the right direction. For some inexplicable reason, I felt that questioning God from the vantage point of someone who is about to die would loosen all inhibitions. It would be as if I were perched atop of Jacob's ladder, with God sitting next to me (*Genesis* 28:12-13). No longer being intimidated by death, eye-to-eye, I would feel free to challenge God. I would have nothing to lose, and, if I came up with some answers, then everything to gain. However, the reader should not have heightened expectations, believing that my search for God will necessarily provide answers to theological questions. As its title states, this book is designed to ask questions; and, as often is the case, one question leads to another.

I know that approaching God with such "deadly" reasoning may seem negatively motivated. Then again, the great medieval Jewish philosopher, Moses Maimonides (1135-1204), developed a theory of "negative theology": One knows who God is by first defining what God is not. If questioning God — **including the very existence of a Higher Being** — helps me to deal in a measured manner with death, then I will be grateful; as will my wife who will be able to sleep peacefully without being awakened in the middle of the night by a panic-stricken husband. I am told that impending death not only prompts questions of one's own life, but also about God's role, or lack thereof, in it. It is at death's door that we are most vulnerable and that we seek answers, so we can be accepting of our fate, secure in the knowledge that our lives had meaning; and, that maybe, just maybe, we were among the thirty-six righteous people.

And so, I am left no alternative, but to begin my story at the end.

The Beginning of the End

It is early Thursday morning, May 27, 2004, about 6:30, exactly two weeks after my sixtieth birthday. My wife stayed the night with me in the hospital, having heard from the doctors that I will, at best, live on for another week to ten days. Assuming that I am deep in a coma, which they have no reason not to believe, they are speaking freely in my presence about my final days, as if I am already dead. *"Chutzpah"*!

However, while I cannot physically respond, I am aware of everything. I am alive, but only within myself. Naturally, I have no idea when I slipped into unconsciousness, as I can only remember the waking periods; and, this is one of them. God, how I want to let them know, to say something, to move a finger or blink an eye. But, nothing. I can emit only a silent cry.

A hazy new day smothers the room, and slowly the outside world lights up my sunken face. In a short time, all my children and grandchildren will come to my room, and begin the process of separating, of saying goodbye. I am not at all sure that I am up for their emotional outpouring, their pain being too great to bear. I am afraid my heart will break before my last breath clothes me in eternal darkness. There is no satisfaction in knowing that your family will miss you so terribly; only a deep sadness, a profound sense of their loss. No ego here, just the mutterings of a father, grandfather and husband who knows what his worth was to his family. Without doing any comparative shopping at an emotional mall, it is hard to believe that my love for them is equaled by their love for me. Nothing unique here. I entered this coma so unexpectedly that I never had a chance to say anything to them. Had I attempted to speak about matters of death when I was healthy, my family would have protested that they did not want to hear of such painful possibilities — not that I would have said anything particularly profound. So, I will leave them without words of wisdom, but hopefully with memories filled with positive values.

As I lie here, I know I must prepare myself for the inevitable; confident that God will accompany me on my new journey into the unknown. To quote the Psalmist: "Even though I walk through the valley of the shadow of death, I will fear no evil, for You, O' God, are with me..." (23:4). Only one problem: God seems to be hiding. I can't see Him or Her (must be politically correct and gender sensitive even when facing death).[1] Okay, I am fully aware that God often seemed to have abandoned me in life, and, maybe I abandoned God as well, but I did expect that the Lord would be present as I approach death — to guide me through it. After all, there is not a more lonely time in one's life than the passage to eternal sleep, even when enwrapped by the warmth of one's family. But, as it correctly says in *Psalms* 89:48: "What person can live and never behold death"? Actually, I was hoping that I would be that one person. To quote Woody Allen: "It's not that I'm afraid to die, I just don't want to be there when it happens"!

I am even considering the Mel Brooks' *Two-Thousand-Year Old Man's* approach to impending death:

> You know how you can avoid the Angel of Death? Before you go
> to sleep at night, eat a pound-and-a-half of garlic. When the

---

1. There is an objective reason to use both the male and female nomenclature for God. In Judaism, while the name God (*Elohim, Adonai*) is in the masculine gender, that which defines God's spiritual being (*Shechina*) is feminine. The same is true in Islam. The name for God (*Allah*) is masculine, but that which defines God's Heavenly core (*Al-Dat*) is feminine.

Angel of Death comes over to you and taps you on the shoulder,
you say: "Whhhhhooo is it"? You heard of the kiss of death. Well,
he's not gonna kiss you. You're full of garlic.

But, as much as I desperately want to postpone my final day, I know
that I will not be able to put it off.

And so, here I lie, ironically, still a believer; and, God? Well, as I
said: Nowhere to be found. What a disappointment. Yet, there is a
silver lining, for as long I can remain in this semi-comatose state,
still half-awake, I will exploit the time that remains to ponder what
is happening at my "moment of truth": To try to find out everything
I wanted to know about God, but was afraid to ask (or didn't have
the time or energy to). As far as I am concerned, God has some
answering to do; and I am not going to let a little thing like my
impending death stand in the way of my asking some questions. If I
do not warrant some answers, then just look around this room — at
my wife, my children and my grandchildren, gathered next to my
bed, crying uncontrollably — they deserve a reasoned response. The
living should merit better treatment than the deceased.

So, I swear, over my soon-to-be dead body, I will get to the
bottom of this so-called God-obsession with which we all struggle.
I will ask some questions about the Almighty. God has left me no
choice.

Is God a *"Figment of Our Imagination"?*

My trip to death is an interesting one. But, before I reveal the beginning of my story, I feel obligated to talk about the "after-story," what I envision as my literal post-mortem, where I hope to continue to talk about my belief in God, or rather, the absence of that belief, or better yet, the confusion of that belief, and God's role in my life; for I have always had a fascination with a Higher Being. After all, I doubt that I will be able to get all the answers to my questions during my remaining days.

But, where to start? Well, did you hear the one about the agnostic dyslexic insomniac who stayed up all night contemplating whether there is a DOG? Theology is a hard nut to crack. In regard to one's belief in a Higher Being, most people fall into the category of being agnostics, not really knowing. Yet, unlike the insomniac, they do not lose much sleep worrying about the whole issue. Colloquially speaking, many are indeed dyslexic when it comes to God — that is, terribly confused.

It has long fascinated me that I always needed more than faith to prod me to believe in God. Belief and faith are not necessarily inter-changeable. One can believe in many things. Faith, however, requires one to hold that his or her beliefs are dependable. I wanted proof. Without evidence of God in my world, my exercise in worship seemed selfish. I was simply using my **imagination** to find comfort. I **imagined** that there was this amorphous Something or Someone to Whom I could turn, knowing full well that God was really a **figment of my imagination**. Not that there is anything wrong with bouncing your thoughts off an invisible partner. After all, we all did that when we were young, whether in the shape of an imaginary friend or a doll. Often, on my long walks, if I did not talk to myself, I would construct conversations with someone else, either real or imagined. The older I became, the more frequent were these self-indulgent tete-a-tetes.

As for prayer, the mode of expression employed to worship God, I used it for introspection. Prayer also made me feel part of a community, thus satisfying my intense need to belong. However, I always believed that the main objective of prayer was to reach God.

I guess I admire the "true believers," be they Jewish, like myself, Christian, Moslem, Hindu, Buddhist, or whatever. If I had their faith, I am certain that I would be handling my fast-approaching death a lot better. But, there are too many things wrong in the world that challenge my belief-system. It is not only the tragedies that are caused by us humans that trouble me, but all those natural and physical disasters. I am not just talking about earthquakes, typhoons, tornadoes, hurricanes, fires, floods and droughts, nor am I talking about those who contract a fatal illness in the prime of their lives, but rather everyday tragedies: My twelve-year old sister being killed in a trolley-car accident, a friend's niece dying in an avalanche of snow while attempting to climb a mountain in Peru, a friend who is suffering from Lou Gehrig's disease, and perhaps most upsetting of all, the premature death of the son of a Holocaust survivor of Auschwitz. If you will pardon the expression, such things kill me.

I know — the true believer quotes *Ecclesiastes*: "Everything has a reason under the sun." What "Godly" reason could there have been for my sister to be crushed to death under the wheels of a trolley-car one bright afternoon? And, even if there were a reason, why should my parents have had to suffer such a tragedy? For certain, no one could expect them to comprehend such an inexplicable event.

Her death is unforgivable, that is, even if we try to justify it in the name of some higher purpose that only God can know. This leads to the claim that it is not for us to question the ways of God, for lowly mortals cannot possibly understand Divine reasoning. If we cannot understand the Divine order of the world, then why should we believe? If we are destined not to make sense out of God's "mysterious ways," how can we possibly believe in some unfathomable Being? The only thing that is incomprehensible is the seemingly utter illogic of this seeming omnipotent-impotent relationship (God-us).

Who can make sense of it? Sure, there are Hegel and Descartes and Kierkegaard and Heidegger and Aristotle and Aquinas and Kant and Luther and Maimonides and Spinoza and Heschel and dozens of more philosophers and theologians. I read them all, including Plato and Moore and Thales and Leibnitz and Pritchard and Whitehead and Buber and Rosenzweig and Cox and Soloveitchik. If you ask the average person, he or she would probably say that what these intellectuals wrote sounds like guesswork — a sort of mental gymnastics, a good exercise for the mind. Despite these luminaries' genuine erudition, they help the average lay person very little. Their philosophical perorations are generally too complicated and too far beyond the understanding of most of us to be of any substantial help. So, we continue to **imagine** what God is like.

Is There only One God?

We read in *Deuteronomy*: "Hear, O' Israel, the Lord our God, the Lord is One" (6:4). I believe in the "Father, Son and Holy Spirit." I believe in the Ahura Mazda. I believe in Allah. And then, there is the ancient Greek God in whom Tiger Woods and Michael Jordan believe (or rather endorse) — Nike: the God of Victory.

The battle against a variation of Persian dualism, which held that there were polar Gods — of darkness and light, of good and bad — was engaged with the entry of Judaism. With the introduction of Abram (Abraham), who is considered the first Jew, it is not at all certain that his monotheism was truly pure as is commonly held. His God seemed to be a tribal one, attached to his geographical wanderings.

To make certain that there would be no confusion between monotheism and any form of multi-theism, when the Jews finally codified their daily prayer book between the seventh and eleventh centuries, the rabbis altered the opening lines of the prayer that speaks of the Creation, which was based on a passage from *Isaiah*: "Who forms light and creates darkness, makes peace and **creates evil**" (47:7). The prayer now reads: "Who forms light and creates darkness, who makes peace and **creates everything**." While darkness is readily associated with suffering and evil, the word "darkness" is more palliative — certainly less definitive — than the word "evil." Of course, no one likes to believe that, while there is one God Who created everything, evil was a part of the Almighty's Creation, unless we can only understand "good" by contrasting it to that which is its opposite. After all, we know that "The Good, The Bad and The Ugly" do exist in our world. With such definitive demarcations, how can there be any truth to the statement: "Opposites attract"?

What of the tripartite system of belief adopted by certain Christian denominations that speaks of the Father, Son and Holy Spirit? According to early Christian doctrine, these divisions of the Godhead actually constitute One God. In Islam, Allah is Supreme and Singular. That He (no doubt here of a male appellation) attracts the masses of His people on holy pilgrimages to three different sacred spots — Mecca, Medina and the Temple Mount (Jerusalem) — does not mean that He is divided into three equal parts.

That each one of the three monotheistic religions seeks redemption through a personal Messiah does not contradict the notion of one God. We all send others on missions on our behalf. The head of a law firm might instruct a junior partner to do some essential research on a client the firm is representing. The President of the United States sends his press secretary to face reporters. Soldiers execute the policies of the country they serve. Why shouldn't God appoint someone else to carry out His or Her will? There is a consistency here that was already established in biblical times, where God often appeared in various disguises, as an angel or a guest. Did not the prophets do God's bidding? And, wasn't Jesus himself simply a messenger of God, a messenger whose status was enhanced by a miraculous story of being born of a virgin? What is wrong with the prophet Elijah mounting a white donkey and riding it over Mount Moriah to usher in a messianic age of peace and prosperity? Maybe God is so humble that He or She wants to give the credit to someone else. And, of course, if the end of days were not to bring down upon us an apocalypse, but rather an era of enlightenment and human decency, then we mortals should welcome it with open arms. Here the messenger is less important than the message.

It would be quite perplexing to believe in more than one God. Juggling too many things at the same time can be self-defeating. An individual must shoulder his or her responsibilities in life and execute them well, but does not need to complicate things with a multiple belief system.

While I will attempt to demonstrate how complex is one's belief in God, all my questions nevertheless have been directed to one address. My natural instinct is to speak to a single God, and I have been forewarned to do so in the first of the Ten Commandments:

> You shall have no other gods besides Me. You shall not make for yourself a sculptured image, or any likeness of what is in the heavens above, or on the earth below, or in the waters under the earth. You shall not bow down to them or serve them. (*Exodus* 20:3-5).

I admit that there are problems with these verses. Who is to say that these other "gods" are false? The entire Ten Commandments are introduced with the words: "I, the Lord, am your God Who brought you out of the land of Egypt." Since the Jews became a nation after they escaped from Egypt into the wilderness of Sinai, where they received the Written and Oral Law (*Torah* and *Talmud*), it becomes obvious that this is the one God Who should be obeyed.

Another challenge with the verse is how one interprets the prohibition of fashioning any image of God. For Jews and Moslems it means that their houses of worship are devoid of replicas that would suggest any likeness of the Deity. In many churches however, stained-glass windows depict images of Jesus, Mary and angels, even as statues of saints adorn the sanctuaries.

Yet, despite these varying interpretations, all three religions subscribe to one God, a single Unity. As a Jew, I see this singularity in what I would call a "unity principle of historical monotheism," which is fueled by a determination to cope with the diversity of the natural order and with the variegation of historical experience as evidence of this Unity.

The powers and the functions of one God have throughout history been expanded to include new experiences, new understandings and new knowledge. This has meant that religious belief has not been committed to a single concept of God, but to a single theory: God must be adequate to deal with natural phenomena, scientific advancement and historical growth. Since religious awareness and experience constantly underwent change, concepts of God were broadened so that God might remain adequate. The idea of one God grew and developed because of a tenacious commitment to the unity principle of historical monotheism.

The personal (almost tribal) God of Abraham was quite different from the national God of Moses, who was significantly different from the messianic God of the rabbis — and all were very different from the God of Christ and Allah. What this all means is that there was and still is only one God, but with varied conceptualizations.

Judaism satisfied this historical belief in one God through episodic and creative syncretism. Exposed to radical shifts in history, it constantly reshaped itself without sacrificing its identity. The Jewish religion became innovative. The outcome of such innovation was always a varied form of the past — not always as a logical outgrowth of previous forms of religious expression, but rather as an historical consequence of having to overcome complex issues of survival. The classic example is found in Rabbinic Judaism. The rabbis of the Common Era fashioned a basically new form of religious understanding that would ease the transition from a self-contained, Temple-based religion of sacrifice as a form of worship to one that would be adaptable to a life of exile, which would embrace prayer in place of ritual sacrifice. (Christianity also evolved, spawning a multitude of Christian denominations.)

Will commitment to God, capable of enveloping the evolution of history, take precedence over **traditional** concepts of God? Or will it find itself impotent in the face of change? Will religion surrender its traditional paradigm of ideological growth and historical development for **tradition**? If it does, then we will be confronted with different gods for different time periods. But, if our theology is understood as progressive, then a single God can span generations, adapting Him- or Herself to changing times, as only a single God could do.

The world is changing rapidly. Technological and scientific advancements, as well as evolving political realities, challenge us to reemphasize a religion whose strength has always been its adaptability. In order to safeguard this flexibility, theology must avoid institutionalizing any alliance between politics and religion. Such an "unholy" alliance only tends to stifle the traditional progression of thought, belief and practice.

To guarantee a continued dynamism of religious belief, God must continue to be traditionally defined as capable of coping with change. If this paradigm of change is no longer essential to religious growth, or perceived as a threat, we will be forced to create many gods. Our understanding of God must countenance a God Who is flexible, creative and viable for our time — **one God** Who will serve us in an ever-changing world.

Question #3 — *Does Everyone Believe in the Same God?*

I often ask myself: Is the God Whom people believe in the same God for everyone? I don't just mean is Allah equal to Jesus who is equal to Buddha who is equal to Yahweh. Do Taoists have the same God as Baha'ists? The Druse do not reveal their beliefs to any outsider, and the Mormons do not allow access to their holy tabernacle to anyone but a card-carrying Mormon. So… who knows what God they believe in? There are different sizes and shapes of Buddhas on virtually every street corner in Kyoto and in everyone's home there. Are they all the one and the same Buddha? Given the privatization of religion, how can we possibly know if the God of Confucianism is the same as the God of Islam?

If each religion has its own God, does that mean that there is more than one God, thus making a mockery of Western religions' notion of monotheism? If I, as a Jew, believe in a God of history, and the guy in the bed next to me believes in the God of the Trinity, then we already have a few Gods floating around — unless he thinks that his God is the only true God, and my God is merely a pretender to the Divine throne. Since the generations have been afflicted with so many religious wars, it is clear that the primacy of one God over another is of some importance. If the Catholics in Northern Ireland were to overwhelm the Protestants there, would that mean that the Protestant God was a false one, or rather an inferior one? For certain, throughout the Old Testament, the God of the Israelites defeats every nation on earth in order to set them up in their Divinely-promised homeland.

Yet, only after a relatively short historical time-frame, the Israelites were driven out of ancient Israel, first by the Babylonians and then by the Romans. Paganism and later Christianity shunted the Israelites' God aside. Does this mean that the Israelites put too many eggs in one Divine basket, that they would have been better off had they hedged their bets, contemplating the growing religious forces around them? Might the Israelites, or the Jews in general, have been better served by history had they abandoned their God, and moved on to other gods, who apparently were more powerful than the One in Whom they had placed their trust? Or, was their faithfulness eventually rewarded when they returned to their ancestral homeland close to two millennia after their dispersion, as promised by God to the progenitor of the Jewish people, Abraham? But, what of the interim two thousand years when Jews were singled out for suffering, and even liquidation, during the Crusades, the Spanish Inquisition and the Third Reich? Did their God go into hiding then, providing for the supremacy of a Christian, Catholic or Aryan God?

If we want to consider ourselves to be true pluralists, tolerant of other people's beliefs and practices, then we would have to acknowledge that everyone serves a different God; or, at the least, that everyone probably prays to a different God. I would wager that that same guy lying next to me, when in church, may not even have addressed the same God as his fellow parishioners. If one observes the behavior patterns of different ardent believers, who all contend that they are following in God's ways, it would appear that lots of people are marching to their own Divine tune. Otherwise, how does one explain the inconsistencies in religious practice, whereby observant Catholics are forbidden to eat fish on Fridays, devout Jews to mix milk and meat products, and a practicing Moslem to eat pork? If God is the same God for everyone, then these prohibitions would be incumbent upon everyone — although such a food embargo would take all the enjoyment out of eating at a good French restaurant.

It would be okay if one's belief in God only required ritual differences of behavior, but when those varied beliefs influence moral behavior, then there could be real trouble, especially when adopted by nations; and here I refer back to religious wars in which countries declare that God is on their side. Too often nationalism and theology have become confused. There is a temptation to enlist the Deity as a weapon in one's national arsenal. Could it be that fundamental Islam motivates the Iranians to develop nuclear capability in order to dominate the world? Does the war between the United States and Iraq signify the approach of Armageddon, where Occidental clashes with Middle Eastern or even Oriental (North Korea)? Are we headed for a clash of civilizations all in the name of my God, or your God, or their God? Which, what and whose God are we talking about?

Most likely, we are talking about a man-made, woman-created God, each God suiting our own definition, or rather our own needs and ideologies as shaped by the society in which we have been raised, or by some unexplained inner eclecticism. How is it possible that Christianity and Judaism, which both accept the biblical account of the Creation, hold such contrasting views of that same God? How is it that Jews and Arabs are at war, when both claim to be descendants of the same father, Abraham? Why does that God of Creation refuse to sort the whole matter out? Does God enjoy this confusion?

While many in the field of religious academia would argue that God is not a variation of the same theme, that God is one and the same God for everyone, this intellectual observation has not penetrated the masses. I could no more feel comfortable joining a revivalist meeting with one of those televangelists than would an

evangelist feel comfortable in my synagogue parading around with a
Torah in hand, chanting some ancient hymn in Hebrew. Each one of
us, while declaring the authenticity of our own system of belief,
might simultaneously decry others'. This is not to say that others
are not entitled to practice what they believe, provided, of course,
that their practice and belief do not intrude on the manner of
practice and belief of someone else.

The fact that my religion demands of me to pray three times a
day, and the religion of the guy a few rooms down the hall demands
of him to pray five times a day, does not necessarily mean that we
are praying to different Gods. It also does not mean that because he
prays twice a day more than I do (actually five times more), he is
superior to me and will be favored by God. After all, we are both
here together on the brink of death. This makes me conclude that
the good person and the bad person face the consequences of their
behavior not because God judges them and metes out rewards and
punishments accordingly, but rather because society sets certain
rules, customs and laws. It is these rules, customs and laws that call
a person to account, or do not, as coincidence or luck or
happenstance plays a decisive role in what comes to pass as a result
of one's behavior and actions.

In Judaism, the morning and evening, Sabbath and Holiday,
services end with this universal appeal:

> Therefore we place our hope in You, O' Lord, our God, that we
> may soon see Your mighty splendor, to remove detestable
> idolatry from the earth, and false gods will be utterly cut off, to
> perfect the universe through the Almighty's sovereignty. Then **all
> humanity will call upon your Name,** to turn all the earth's wicked
> toward you. **All the world's inhabitants will recognize and know
> that to You every knee must bend and every tongue pay
> homage... and they will all accept the yoke of Your rulership** that
> You may reign over them soon and eternally. For the kingdom is
> Yours and You will reign for all eternity in glory, as it is written in

Your *Torah*: "The Lord will reign for all eternity" (*Exodus* 15:18). And it is said: "**The Lord will be Ruler over all the world** — on that day the Lord will be One and His Name Shall be One" (*Zechariah* 14:9).

This universal dictate overwhelms the more particular aspects of the prayer book. Even though this prayer grows out of a Jewish liturgical context, its spiritual message is that there is only one God for all humanity, though there may be a multiplicity of religious approaches to that singular Divine Entity.

Does it matter if we believe in the same God or not? I would argue that the answer to this rather perplexing issue is that each person chooses his or her own manner of practice and belief to reach the same God. God is the constant in this entire discussion. While we may not be able to say definitively that God is always the same, we can say that we human beings are most certainly not the same, which explains our conflicting behavior and actions.

Can God Contradict Him- or Herself?

If God is truly One, then we should expect some manner of consistency in His or Her behavior; and yet, contradictions seem to abound in religious texts. For example, Jews read in their morning prayers:

> Blessed are You, O' God, Ruler of the Universe, Who has formed human beings in wisdom and created in them manifold orifices and cavities. It is revealed and known before the throne of Your glory that if one of them be opened, or one of them be closed, it would be impossible to keep alive and stand before Your countenance.

Well, if that is the case, and God knows this to be true, then that would explain why many people are dying right and left — because a particular organ in their body failed to function as it should. When this particular prayer closes with the words, "Blessed be You, O' God, Healer of all flesh and doing wonders," whom are we kidding? The healer of all flesh is Dr. Gynecologist or Dr. Bile Duct or Dr. Colon. I might have been better off placing my faith in Dr. Liver than in Dr. God, although, given my present situation, you would never know that.

Indeed, the theological contradictions that exist within the Bible are so manifold that it is impossible to make heads or tails out of God's actions. Which is the correct creation story? The one which tells us that Eve was created from Adam's rib, or the one that both man and woman were created together, at the same time? Let me be more specific.

In the first chapter of *Genesis*, we read:

> And God said: "Let us make Adam in our own image, in our likeness..." So, God created Adam in the Divine image — in the image of God did the Almighty create him, male and female did God create them (1:26-27).

In the second chapter of *Genesis*, as part of the same biblical narrative, we read:

> And God formed Adam from the dust of the earth and blew into his nostrils the breath of life and Adam became a living soul... Then the Lord God caused a heavy sleep to overcome Adam, and as he slept God took one of his ribs and then closed up his flesh. And the Lord God fashioned the rib that was taken from Adam into a woman (2:7, 21-22).

Which one to believe, if either? Is this allegory or fact? If the entire legend of the creation of humankind is some sort of metaphor, why deliberately sow such confusion?

How about this Divine contradiction? In the *Talmud*, concerning the ancient Israelite exodus from Egypt, it is stated that God upbraids the Israelites for rejoicing after the drowning of their enemies, the Egyptians, in the Red Sea:

> Are these people not part of My Creation? Are you to rejoice at the suffering of others (*Sanhedrin* 39b)?

How can this be? After all, the guiding hand of the Divine Presence was directly felt as God provided for the escape from Egyptian slavery by splitting the sea in the first place, only to purposely close it once the Egyptians were caught in the middle.

And, if we are already speaking of that time in ancient history, then the question that begs to be asked is: If God is omnipotent and omniscient, why couldn't He or She devise a better plan to free the Israelites from Egyptian slavery than killing all the Egyptian first-born boys? Why could God not cause a great sleep to descend upon the Egyptians, not unlike the one that God caused to fall upon Adam before a rib was wrenched from his body to form Eve? If there is a God, it sounds as if He or She is pretty sadistic. How could anyone believe in such a God? By the way, I am not just asking these questions because I will die before my time is up, at least according to my intellectual and emotional clock. Nor am I posing these queries because I am upset that I am going to die relatively young, and so want to get back at God, in the manner that Elie Wiesel did when he recited the *Kaddish* (the Jewish mourning prayer), that praises God, thus trying to make God feel guilty for the horrors of the Holocaust and the deaths of his family at the time. These are simply curiosities that boggle the mind.

One must acknowledge that these contradictions have been addressed by both biblical scholars and religious commentators. Traditional Jewish thought believes in Divine Revelation. The *Torah* — also referred to as the *Five Books of Moses* (*Genesis, Exodus, Leviticus, Numbers, Deuteronomy*) — was given to Moses by God at the top of Mount Sinai. Moses wrote each word down, and what was recorded became immutable fact. Any contradictions that exist in the biblical text are explained in the plethora of traditional Jewish commentaries, particularly the *Talmud* — all of which have a Divine immutability to them.

For those who are involved in biblical criticism, the answer to many of these contradictions lies in the fact (for them) that different parts of the Bible were written at different times by different authors. This has become known as "Higher Criticism," coined by Julius Wellhausen (1844-1918), a German professor of theology. Wellhausen divided the *Torah* into four parts, designating each part to a different author based on the content and/or theme of the biblical text; and giving each one a name (Yahwist, Elohim, Deuteronomic, Priestly) to characterize its particular literary bent. (To be fair, Wellhausen's critical approach to biblical interpretation was preceded by the Jewish philosopher Baruch Spinoza, 1632-1677, who questioned the Divine authorship of the *Torah*.)

The basis of "Higher Criticism" is that the biblical texts are a compilation of diverse sources compiled over hundreds of years, contradicting Moses singular role in the writing of the *Torah*. Indeed, most modern biblical scholars contend that Ezra the Scribe (fourth century B.C.E.) should be considered the major author and editor of the *Torah* as well as of the books of *Joshua*, *Judges*, *Samuel*, and *Kings*.

Yet, for those less schooled in this intellectual/religious debate regarding who wrote the *Torah*, thus trying to explain (away) God's sometimes peculiar behavior, we remain with contradictions that leave us unsettled — contradictions that go well beyond the biblical world and reach deep into our present reality, which will be discussed in subsequent questions. And so, we continue to seek answers to life's mysteries, all the while expecting some consistency and reliability to Divine actions.

Does God have a Split-Personality?

I guess it is possible that God can abide a split-personality. Perhaps, a little bifurcation is good for the soul. Is it conceivable that God's personality is governed by fantasies and delusions? If so, this would explain why God's behavior often seems out of touch with reality, resulting in unpredictable and irrational Divine thoughts and actions. Why not be a God Who is both merciful and vengeful, or a God of peace and war? Being a God of war is most certainly problematic, considering how many wars throughout the ages have been waged in the name of God, or to put it more succinctly, considering how many people have been killed in the name of God. But, there it is, in black and white, on the pages of the Bible. The Israelites are quoted as singing praises to God for guiding them from Egyptian slavery to freedom:

> Then Moses and the Israelites sang this song to the Lord. They said: "I will sing to the Lord, for He has triumphed gloriously; horse and driver, He has hurled into the sea. The Lord is my strength and my might; He is become my salvation. This is my God, and I will enshrine Him, the God of my ancestors, and I will exalt Him. **The Lord is a man of war** — the Lord is His name" (*Exodus* 15:1-3).

Of course, if one believes that the Bible was written by human beings, a redaction by many people, stories passed on from one generation to the next, then all the contradictions in the biblical narrative are understandable. However, if one believes that what is written in the Bible is incontrovertible fact, words uttered by God to a most faithful stenographer, Moses, on the top of Mount Sinai, at a moment of Divine Revelation, then there is a real challenge. Here we are thrust back to the conflict between biblical criticism and religious purity as outlined at the conclusion of the previous question.

Even if a war needed to be waged to extricate the Israelites from bondage, the manner in which God implemented a Divine exit strategy strikes one as unnecessarily brutal — killing all the first-born Egyptian males. If this is Divine example, then I for one do not want any part of it. One would think that God would at least show us how to maintain some sense of moral restraint when going off to battle for a just cause. One is reminded of that wonderful statement in *Deuteronomy*, where God commands us: "Justice, justice, you shall pursue..." (16:20). Why is the word justice used twice? Because we are to pursue a just cause by just means. This is a perfect example of Divine contradiction: God carrying out a just cause in freeing the Israelites from enslavement by unjust means, by killing babies! How can God be so sure of Him- or Herself? Usually, when it comes to competing methods, God is certainly definitive in choosing one over the other.

It would be nice if we could be witness to a little Divine subtlety, rather than this "all or nothing" approach. Since God is considered the very best military strategist, we should expect to see the Almighty designing for us a game plan whereby nations can achieve their goals with a minimum amount of suffering caused to the other side.

Many of us live contradictory lives, with contending values. It is true that things are not black and white, that choices we make are not easily compartmentalized. Often we are confronted with excruciating choices that pose contrasting moral dilemmas, without any one right or wrong response. Perplexity is part of the human psyche. But, who would have expected Divine confusion, unless God is setting up a paradigm for normative human behavior? If divergent behavior patterns are good enough for God, then they should be good enough for us. But, if God is trying to tell us that anything resembling schizophrenia is good for the soul, why are schizophrenics so terribly lost in this world?

How Did God Decide to Create the World and Human Beings in Their Present Form?

It is difficult to go through life and not believe in a Higher Being. The magnificence of the world order is so overwhelming that it is impossible not to ponder the wonder of it all. It is only natural to ask: Who thought of all this? Sun, moon, sky, trees, animals, human beings; and all the concomitant attributes — yellow and red (sun), full and half (moon), blue or gray (skies), elm, pine, oak (trees), alligators, eagles, possums (species), black or white or yellow or red (human beings)? Scientific "Big Bang" theories never really work, because the lingering question begs to be asked: Who or what set off the Big Bang?

Life is a mystery, and mysteries are the wonder of every age. We are intrigued by them. We love mysteries. From the tiniest child to the eldest among us. The child asks the magician: "How did you do that?", hoping that if the magician would move a little slower or let us get a closer look, somehow the magic would be demystified. Most mysteries are solved through observation and knowledge. If we could just see a little more, read a little more, we would understand. If you play the game of *Clue* long enough, it becomes obvious that there was simply never any question that it was Colonel Mustard in the library with the lead pipe...

For all those questions and enigmas that various methods of investigation cannot solve, sometimes maturity can be counted on to come to the rescue. As we grow older and garner more experience and wisdom, oftentimes, later in life, we do understand that which we did not comprehend in our youth. Indeed, how many times, as children, did we hear from our elders: "Listen to the voice of experience," and how many times did we say this to our children? But, there are some mysteries that cannot be solved with more information or more time. The more we experience life's events, the more we realize how much we do not know, and the deeper many of life's secrets become.

And so, the mystery of the world's creation and the fashioning of humankind defies explanation. Experience, knowledge and time are unable to solve life's ultimate question: Is there a God? The best we can do is to imagine (there's that word again — "imagination") that there is something or someone beyond our human understanding who began the whole process that we know as the Creation. Yet, even if our logic would allow us to buy such an incredible story as that which is recorded in the Bible, what follows, in terms of God's behavior, makes little sense. Why would God create a world only to see it fall asunder so quickly in the Garden of Eden, at its truly incipient stage? If one were to attach to God such attributes as good and merciful and forgiving, perhaps one should add the attribute of cynicism; for only a cynic would create an idyllic environment, and place in its midst the potential for disaster. Again, the contradictions stagger the mind.

And yet, we are still obsessed with figuring out how it all began. Who could have thought of the incredible inner machinations of the human species? For example, sex. To think that a few tiny spermatozoa hitting another fews tiny eggs could produce a human being is simply mind-boggling. I know that God is asexual, however, I cannot help but be curious: How did God ever conceive of human beings deriving such physical ecstasy at the moment of orgasm? Did God Him- or Herself experience such tactile intimacy with the opposite sex? Why did not the account of the Creation include something on this subject? After all, procreation is the life-blood of human perpetuity! Why do we not read: "Man and woman delighted in their sexual encounter. God declared that it was very good. And, there was evening and there was morning an 'eighth day?'" After all, according to the Jewish tradition, it is a *mitzvah*, a Divine commandment, for a husband and wife to have sexual intercourse on the seventh day, the Sabbath, when God rested.

And what about a good old-fashioned sneeze, or bathroom needs? Why is there a need for bowel movements or urination? Why do we breathe through our nose and mouth, and not through our ears? Why do we see with our eyes and not with our nose? Speaking of eyes, wouldn't one eye be more efficient? Don't give me the Cro-Magnon, Neanderthal or ape theories, for they only introduce a concept of derivatives. They do not explain the "why" of the matter. Why ten toes and ten fingers — especially when toes are generally so ugly? Doctors can explain some of the physical aspects of our bodies, both the inner and outer parts thereof, but if God is Who He or She is by definition, as One Who can do anything, He or She could have created a different physical being? All that the scientific and medical experts can do is explain the workings of the human body after the fact; that is, after the act of the creation of human beings in the state that we were created. They cannot explain why we were created in the form that we are.

Considering this observation, it strikes me as ironic that so many ideological non-believers stem from the scientific and medical professions. One would expect that, with their vast knowledge of the human body, they would marvel at its intricacies to such an extent that they would buy into the notion of a God, or at least, of "firsts" or of "beginnings." The concept of "creation *ex nihilo*" should be quite consistent with their scientific data and medical discoveries. They should be the first to admit that there does not necessarily have to be a contradiction between their world of hard facts and the believer's world of creative fantasy (or imagination). Each can abide the other. Science and religion are not mutually exclusive.

How Should We Address and/or Describe God?

Why do we use the term He or She for God (almost exclusively "He")? Maybe such nomenclature is completely erroneous. Maybe God is an It, an indefinable "Blob." I do not mean this in any derogatory sense. Perhaps we are all wrong in trying to refer to the Almighty in gender-recognized terms. I know that language has its limitations, and when relating to God we use language almost metaphorically, and certainly poetically. But, can't we go beyond that? Are we incapable of believing in a God who has no human-like features or traits, a God who has no human-like emotions or feelings?

> I believe with complete faith that the Creator, Blessed is His Name, is not physical and is not affected by physical phenomena and that there is no comparison whatsoever to Him (Maimonides' *Thirteen Articles of Faith*).

And yet, we seem compelled to attribute anthropomorphic characteristics to God — God's "open arms" and "outstretched hands." When children are asked to draw a picture of God, they invariably draw an old man, with a long white beard, sitting on some Heavenly throne. When we refer to God as good or merciful or long-suffering or vengeful or redeeming, are we barking up the wrong tree in attaching such elements of the human personality to His or Her Being? Why not exploit this opportunity to expand our language?

And then, there is the definition of God as given by the twentieth century Jewish theologian, Abraham Joshua Heschel (1907-1972), who referred to God as the "Ineffable" — beyond words, indefinable, unspeakable, indescribable, inexpressible. In short, incapable of being known! If we take into account that God has no physical description or definition, then He or She could not have made it any more difficult for us to find Him or Her. If that is the case, then why not just refer to God as a God of "smurgle," or a God of "umbranchence," or a God of "mentaniousness," that is, a God of "gobbeldygook"?

In short, it would be a lot easier to accept God not being a God of good or of mercy, because then we would not always have to decipher why there is so much evil in the world, or why, as Harold Kushner asks in his moving book, *When Bad Things Happen to Good People*, bad things actually do happen to good people. Perhaps we should reverse the order and ask: Why do "good things happen to bad people"? For example, my next door neighbor, who is one of the most deplorable human beings I know, is still going strong at the age of eighty-five, and here I am, just past sixty, a model citizen, waiting for my life to end. So, I would prefer not to refer to God as a God of evenhandedness, for that clearly seems not to be the case, but rather as a God of "crunchlickalolity," because I have no idea what it means, and, therefore cannot fault God for my own misfortune.

This last statement is clearly problematic, because to believe what I wrote means that God really has nothing to do with my present condition, which may mean that God had little, if anything, to do with my life. I am a bit tired to enter into this line of thought right now, but I will have to deal with this at some point. After all, I would hate to think that God played no role whatsoever in my life. This is too existential a thought for me to digest at this moment. So, I will return to this when the so-called "spirit" moves me.

Question #8	*What Constitutes*
	Divine Personality Traits?

It is one thing to believe in God, it is another matter entirely to define the God we believe in. How are we to understand God's personality traits, and know whether they have rubbed off on us? What adjectives do we use to help us understand the very nature of God's being? Can we use human descriptions and apply them to something which is essentially "non-human"?

Perhaps it is best to again employ Maimonidean "negative theology," first describing the personality traits God does not possess, and then, by a process of elimination, conclude what characteristics God does display. Of course, this may prove difficult because, apparently, God acts in ways that parallel our own behavior. In fact, when God exhibits some traits that we would like to believe are reserved for us humans — vindictiveness, pettiness and downright nastiness — God does it on a grand scale. (And so does humankind at times, as evidenced by Hitler's vendetta against the world, exacted primarily on the Jews of Europe.)

I suspect it would be best, therefore, not to dwell on such traits as goodness and justice, compassion and righteousness, unless we speak of them in absolute terms, not relative ones. For example, at the beginning of the story of Noah and the Ark, Noah is described as being: "...righteous and whole-hearted in his generation" (*Genesis* 6:9). In other words, at another time, Noah might have been considered to be a complete moral degenerate. Indeed, his decadence is described after the flood, lending credence to the view that "he was righteous in his generation" only:

> Noah, the tiller of the soil, was the first to plant a vineyard. He drank wine and became drunk, and he uncovered himself in his tent. Ham [one of Noah's sons], the father of Canaan, saw his father's nakedness and told his brothers outside. But, Shem and Japheth [Noah's other two sons] took a cloth, placed it against both their backs and, walking backwards, they covered their father's nakedness; their faces were turned the other way, so that they did not see their father's nakedness (*Genesis* 9:20-23).

While our values and personality traits are measured on a scale that can vary from day to day, Godly characteristics cannot be subjected to similar limitations; that is, not if we want to have faith in a God Who is "perfect," not when compared to others, but on an absolute scale. Less than an absolute approach to the Deity will necessarily diminish God's worth.

My problem is that, as I lie here, God is very diminished in my eyes — not only because I am still upset at what is happening to me, something to which I have yet to reconcile myself, even after asking but a few theological questions — but mainly because I can hear the earth rumble around me, not just in preparation for some terrible physical act of nature, like an earthquake, but because "nations are lifting up sword against nations." Having said this, I am becoming more convinced that if I did have to choose one or even two personality traits above all others that would describe God, and which have remained consistent throughout the generations of humankind, it would be: "inconsistency," and perhaps, "hypocrisy."

We read in *Isaiah*:

> And it shall come to pass, at the end of days, that the mountain of the Lord's house shall be established as the top of the mountains, and shall be exalted above the hills; and all nations

shall flow to it... And God will teach us in His ways, and we will walk in His paths... And He shall judge between the nations, and shall decide for many peoples; and they shall beat their swords into plowshares, and their spears into pruning-hooks; nation shall not lift up sword against nation, neither will they learn war anymore (2:2-4).

If this be the case, then why was I standing with 300,000 fellow Americans in Washington, DC, in 1969 at the protest against the war in Vietnam? Why only thirteen years later, in 1982, did I join 400,000 Israelis in Tel Aviv's city square to protest the war in Lebanon? Why am I still singing: "I'm gonna lay down my sword and shield, down by the riverside — ain't gonna study war no more"? I don't get it. Is Isaiah's prophecy, in God's name, to come true only at the end of days; and, to hasten the end of days, nations are to do the exact opposite of what will be at the end of days? Have you ever heard of such perverted logic? How inconsistent and hypocritical can God be? Why could not God send Isaiah to institute his prophecy for immediate implementation? Why delay it for who knows when? Maybe what God meant was, at the rate that nations are lifting up swords against nations, at the end of days, there will be no more nations; that is – no nation will be able to lift up swords against nations. God just seems to give us one major Excedrin headache.

So, what constitutes Divine traits? To return to the notion of negative theology, let us try to figure out what it is that we do not want God to possess. Well, for starters, how about hypocrisy and inconsistency. Let us exclude any trait that we would not like to see present in ourselves, such as greed, self-aggrandizement, selfishness, jealousy, resentment, bitterness or hatred. Let us also rule out any trait that has a finality to it, like "Terminator," "Conan, the Barbarian," "Predator" and all manner of Arnold Schwarzeneggerisms, that is ones that can wipe the earth off the face of the universe.

Now that we know what traits we do not want God to have, what characteristics are we able to live with? How about holy? "God is Holy." We hear that expression all the time. What could it possibly mean? Sacred, blessed, divine, spiritually pure, consecrated, hallowed, awesome, amazing and miraculous? For certain, "holy" does not apply to us, accept as a derivative, as in: He or she is a "holy person." If anyone wanted a definition of God, he or she would probably use the word "holy," because, like God, it seems beyond definition. God refers to Him- or Herself as Holy: "I, the Lord your God, am Holy." I guess we would not apply the personality trait of humility to God.

If holy means all those attributes defined above, from sacred to miraculous, all of which have an absolute quality to them, then it becomes clear that God possesses traits that are far beyond us, but which we should strive to emulate. For certain, the biblical Holiness Code does provide us with a Divine standard of behavior — to care for the widow, the orphan, the stranger who lives among us (see *Leviticus* 19:1-37). But, if we were to relate again to the big four positive traits of goodness, justice, righteousness and compassion, we would have to say that, while we are good, God is Goodness; while we are just, God is Justice; while we are righteous, God is Righteousness; and while we are compassionate, God is Compassion. We are the adjectives, mere appendages of Divine nouns.

Do such absolute personality traits help to solidify one's belief in God? Not necessarily, but they do provide a system of high expectations. If God is **absolutely** this, that or the other Thing, then we expect the **absolute** best from the Almighty. And judging from my rather lowly position, I have yet to see God's best. What good is it to be the best, if you can't "stand and deliver"?

What are God's Powers?

According to the three monotheistic religions, God is all-powerful. I would like to offer up a theory of what I call: "The Unused Potential of the Divine Power of God."

Hebrew grammar plays an important role in Jewish theology, in part because of its seven verbal conjugations — one of them possessing causative value. In the defining set of benedictions in the daily Jewish liturgy — known simply as the *Tefilah* (prayer), or *Avodah* (worship), or *Sh'moneh Esrei* (eighteen benedictions) — a Jew gives testimony to God's power.

> You are eternally mighty, My Lord, the Resuscitator of the dead are You, abundantly able to save. God sustains the living with kindness, resuscitates the dead with abundant mercy, supports the fallen, heals the sick, releases the confined, and maintains faith to those asleep in the dust. Who is like you, O' Master of mighty deeds, and who is comparable to You, O' King, Who causes death and restores life and makes salvation sprout. And You are faithful to resuscitate the dead. Blessed are You, HaShem [the name of God], **Who causes the dead to come alive.**

I am sure that the codifiers of the prayer book would want all worshippers to interpret this prayer not just metaphorically, but also literally. What is important to note here is the conjugational change that takes place in the original Hebrew of this prayer: "God who resuscitates the dead." In the very last line, the verb, "resuscitate," changes conjugations from the *Pi'el* (emphatic) to *Hif'il* (causative). And so, we recite: "**God who causes the dead to come alive.**"

Surely the reader can understand why I would be so fond of this particular blessing. I know that I have a myopic view of the world now, which is admittedly egocentric, but, if those who codified the prayer book wanted to get across the notion that God is indeed all-powerful, capable of doing the impossible, then they could have chosen no better example for us mortals. Since birth and death are so awesome in human consciousness and understanding, anyone who can return the dead to life must indeed possess absolute power.

Comedian Mel Brooks' *Two-Thousand-Year Old Man* explains it like this, when asked by Carl Reiner:

> **Reiner:** Did you live before man believed in the Almighty?
>
> **2000:** Oh, yeah, a few years before. A couple of years.
>
> **Reiner:** Did you believe in anything? Did you believe in any Superior Being?
>
> **2000:** Yes, a guy — Phil.
>
> **Reiner:** Who was Phil?
>
> **2000:** Phillip. The leader. The leader of our tribe.
>
> **Reiner:** What made him the leader?
>
> **2000:** Very big. Very strong. A big beard, a big chest, and big arms. I mean, he could kill you. He could just walk on you and you could die.
>
> **Reiner:** And you revered him?
>
> **2000:** We prayed to him. Would you like to hear one of our prayers to Phillip?
>
> **Reiner:** Could you remember these prayers?

2000: "Ohhhh, Phillip. Please don't take our eyes out and don't pinch us and don't hurt us. Ohhhhhh. Aaaaamen." That was it.

Reiner: And Phillip did these things?

2000: Yes.

Reiner: And you followed him?

2000: Right.

Reiner: How long was his reign?

2000: Oh, not too long. Not too long. Because one day Phillip was hit by lightning.

Reiner: Aaahh.

2000: And we looked up, we said: "There's something bigger than Phil-il-l"!

Reiner: So, you gave up on Phillip.

2000: Yes.

Reiner: And you started to pay allegiance to that new God.

2000: Yes, to the new Lord.

Reiner: You didn't call him Lord then?

2000: No. The first name we had for him, I think, was "Gevalt." Gevalt! I mean with that lightning, we were already gevalt! Wow!

Believe me, if, in one of their Las Vegas hotel acts, illusionists Siegfried and Roy could move from taming tigers to bringing Las Vegas icon Liberace back to life, they would warrant the prayer: "O' Sigmund, O' Roy, praised be Your names." Of course, after Roy was mauled by one of his tigers, I would simply say: "There's something bigger than Roy"!

If, at a funeral, a person were suddenly to rise from the casket, stating that God had given him back life, there would be an incredible increase in believers, not to mention that religious institutional attendance would grow dramatically (and hospitals would be filled with people being treated for shock).

Yet, we all know — even if we believe that God is capable of such a dramatic feat as reviving a dead person — that God has yet to activate this unused potential of the Divine power; that is, if we restrict the proof of God's power to the example as given in the prayer book, of restoring life to someone who has already expired. I realize that the resurrection of Jesus is the exception, but, as a Jew, I do not believe in the advent of Christ's Second Coming. It should be enough to accept the creation of the world (*ex nihilo*) as proof of God's omnipotence. But, somehow, we are always searching for further substantiation, as we already take the creation of the world as a given.

Now, we might want to ask: Why does God not implement this limitless power? Is it a matter of population control? Or does it have something more to do with the natural order of things — that is, the cycle of life and death. Death creates the possibility for new life (or does it?). But, if God does have absolute power, could not the Almighty have devised a more orderly system, whereby every human being lived until a specific age, at which time he or she would then simply close his or her eyes and enter eternal rest?

Does God Possess Healing Powers?

Let us assume for the moment that any conflict that exists between science and theology is resolved. If so, what would prevent one from believing in God? Nothing, except for the fact that so much of belief in God seems to stretch the imagination, and to turn common sense on its head. For instance, televangelism. What is that all about? Everyone seems so terribly gullible. This "laying of the hands" on someone suffering from a chronic disease in order to heal him or her seems like an exercise in Divine magic. Then again, maybe there is something to this sort of mystical wizardry. After all, God turns rods into snakes and rivers into blood. But that is God Who did it, not Preacher "X" or "Y," who is interrupted every fifteen minutes by a TV commercial for American Express or Royal Crown Cola.

As presented on the evangelical TV programs, a wheelchair-bound guy suddenly able to sprint a four-minute mile, or some seventy-year old blind woman unexpectedly able to read an optometrist's eye chart from a hundred yards away, defies all logic. There is little question that one's mental and emotional state, as well as one's faith, can create the conditions for a positive attitude that can go a long way in aiding the healing process, but usually, any healing that does occur is a coincidence; and, in the case of these wondrous TV preacher/healers, we are often talking about outright fraud.

There seems to be something terribly false about praying to God for a negative result of a liver biopsy, when the outcome is predetermined prior to the biopsy. No manner of prayer is going to change the results. And yet, it is only natural that we would rejoice at a negative finding. After all, that is what every patient hopes for. A biopsy is necessary to provide an accurate diagnosis for proper treatment. Then again, if one's faith is so certain that the results will be good, then one should thank God beforehand! Of course, we would not need God to activate any healing powers if He or She had not created the illness, or the potential for sickness, in the first place!

And yet, within the Jewish tradition, the "prayer for the sick," which is essentially a prayer for healing, is given Divine force by the blessing in the daily prayer book:

> You are eternally mighty, My Lord… abundantly able to save…
> Who supports the fallen and **heals the sick**…

During the reading of the *Torah* in synagogue, a blessing for healing is added. Indeed, within the Reform Jewish movement, this insertion of a special prayer for the ill has reached mythic proportions, as the rabbi turns to the congregants and instructs them, as his or her gaze descends upon them, to call out a name of someone they know who is afflicted with some sort of disease. After that, as one voice, they sing the special prayer for those who are in need of physical and/or emotional healing. As a rabbi, I have often invoked this prayer when I knew that the person who was reciting a blessing before reading the *Torah* had a family member who was ailing.

In Israel, when visiting the grave of a great Jewish sage or personality, one might encounter people praying for the recovery of someone who has been stricken with an illness. Brightly colored scarfs are placed on the grave — the idea being that these dazzling colors, aided by the force of the individual buried there, will fend off the "evil eye," which has cast its spell of sickness upon a loved one. (Taking a page out of Jewish mysticism, pop diva Madonna wears a red ribbon to ward off the evil spirit.) The only problem is that it all seems too "voo-doo" like.

Do any of these people believe that such prayerful incantations will actually save someone from a certain fate? Some perhaps do, some don't. But, tremendous comfort is derived from such worshipful entreaties, not only by the person who is actually contending with an illness, but also by his or her family and friends. It is very natural to pray fervently when we are in tremendous physical pain, to hope against hope. And, indeed there are surprises, as in the case of my rabbinic colleague who was given no more than six months to live, and for whom a farewell party was organized. Over ten years later, he is very much alive, vibrant and active. Perhaps this falls into the category of miracles.

There are definite advantages to believing in God's healing power; but, what if our fervent prayers fail us? Could it be that such prayers can lead one to avoid confronting reality, so that we are psychologically ill-prepared to face certain death or a debilitating illness? After all, it is wise to "put one's house in order" before departing from this world. This refers not only to making amends for past transgressions, but also, and primarily, to helping one's family prepare for a future life without us, emotionally **and** financially.

For the majority of us, beseeching God to exercise Divine healing powers is simply an instinctive reaction. It offers reassurance. While it can provide hope, it need not create false optimism; for most of us are realistic enough to understand the limitations of Divine intervention.

Can Anyone Communicate with God?

If we cannot find the language to define God, or to describe God, or to talk to God, then of what use is religious belief? Of course, there are the Hari Krishna types, who seem to communicate with a Higher Being in some indiscernible tongue that one can never be sure God could understand. However, since God "confused" the tongues of everyone during the time of the Tower of Babel (*Genesis* 11:1-9) so that seventy odd nations, when trying to communicate, sounded one to the other as if speaking gibberish, it can be assumed that God can understand Swahili and Polish and Arabic and English.

What about a deaf-mute? Can God hear the silent longing of an individual who cannot speak? Do we really need the poetic insertions crafted into thousands of prayer books in hundreds of languages to express our faith in God? If so, what is a blind person to do, who does not have access to a prayer book in Braille? Is there a secret code, a unique formulation of words, a special incantation, that increases the chances for Divine communication? Is intent and seriousness of purpose all that are needed?

There is a wonderful Hasidic tale:

When the great Rabbi Israel Baal Shem Tov (Israel Ben Eliezer, c. 1700-1760, the founder of Hasidism) saw misfortune threatening the Jews, it was his custom to go into a certain part of the forest to meditate. There he would light a fire, say a special prayer, and the miracle he begged for would be accomplished.

Later, when his disciple, the celebrated Magid of Mezritch, had occasion, for the same reason, to intercede with heaven, he would go to the same place in the forest and say: "Master of the Universe, listen! I do not know how to light the fire, but I am still able to say the prayer." And, again the miracle would be accomplished.

Still later, Rabbi Moshe Leib of Sasov, in order to save his people once more, would go into the forest and say: "I do not know how to light the fire, I do not know the prayer, but I know the place, and this must be sufficient." It was sufficient and the miracle was accomplished.

Then it fell to Rabbi Israel of Rizhyn to overcome misfortune. Sitting in his armchair, his head in his hands, he spoke to God: "I am unable to light the fire and I do not know the prayer; I cannot even find the place in the forest. All I can do is tell the story, and this must be sufficient." And, it was sufficient.

This touching parable debunks the theories of all those who would have us believe that only the trained religious leader can lead us to communicate with God. Of course, it could be that God created human beings because He or She loves stories!

Yet, there is a difficult reality with which we must contend, for, at least within Judaism, there is no record of anyone communicating directly with God, in the manner that Abraham, Moses, or the prophets did, since the days of the prophet Malachi (literally — "my messenger"), of whom little is known, including the dates of his prophecy. His prophecy closes the biblical section called the Minor Prophets. He proclaimed the universal rule of God (*Malachi* 1:11).

We must ask ourselves: Why did the intimate dialogue that took place between God and God's emissaries cease at the end of the prophetic period, with Malachi? Indeed, throughout history there have been many false prophets who claimed to speak in God's name. And, while in some religions there is a spiritual hierarchy, especially in the Catholic church, rare is the religious leader who would claim that only he or she has the formula to reach God. This is just as well, but nevertheless it leads to the next obvious question: Do we need an intermediary to talk to God?

Do We Need an Intermediary to Talk to God?

The issue that we must deal with is not only whether anyone can communicate with God, but also, whether we need to go through intermediaries. Do we need a mediator to do our Divine bidding? If one looks at organized religion, it seems that access to God must go through a very carefully refined sieve, whose sifter is the priest, the minister, the rabbi, the kadi, the monk — not to mention, for many, the most awesome interlocutor of them all: Jesus Christ. Most certainly in biblical times, there was the High Priest who arranged the sacrificial offerings, the form of worship then, whereby an individual showed his or her allegiance to and belief in God. As for the prophets, God spoke through them. They were the ones who were to deliver God's severe warnings to those nations that acted in immoral ways.

We read of God's "ministering angels." We are taught that God supposedly spoke through the apostles; and now presumably through the Dalai Lama, or possibly through Pat Robertson and Jerry Falwell. The question is: In this technologically advanced world, where communication is conducted within milliseconds, why do we seem to need an old-fashioned operator to place our calls to God? Can't our e-mails be direct? Are we so unsure of ourselves that we need a go-between? Is it that we are uncertain of the language that must be employed? Could it be that we are so awed by the possibility of addressing God, that we lack confidence, that we fear saying something inappropriate that could invite the Holy wrath? Do we think that this is the way it always has been — an intermediary to interpret before God the prayers of human beings? (There is actually an office in Jerusalem where one can fax a message to be placed by a rabbi in the Western Wall, the only physical remnant of the Second Temple.)

Certainly at the beginning of the biblical narrative of the Old Testament, in both the allegorical and historical tales that are recorded, God enters into a dialogue with human beings. It is true that sometimes God appears in a disguise, such as a snake, a wandering stranger, an angel, even once talking through a mule; but for the most part, we see Abraham and Moses speaking directly to God.

Most of us would accept the position that no intermediaries are required when communicating with God, with the possible exception of the Catholic Church, whose hierarchy can be somewhat difficult to navigate: Pope, cardinal, bishop, priest. But, since the notion of "original sin" is an integral part of Catholic theology, it is entirely possible that there is a subconscious fear that the ordinary parishioner is not pure enough to enter into a direct dialogue with God; thus the *raison d'etre* for the confessional booth. But, even here, I would imagine that rare is the priest who would preach that his worshippers not attempt to engage God directly. After all, the prime purpose of prayer is to provide language to facilitate direct communication between God and the worshipper.

The fact of the matter is that it is the most natural thing in the world to call upon God, particularly when we seem incapable of finding a solution to a problem that arises. Also, when one is in situations of stress or danger, there seems to be an inner compulsion that forces the words "God, help me" to emanate from our mouths. As for the oft-cited statement "there are no atheists in foxholes," this will be discussed in the next question and be examined along with the anti-theological thesis that atheism propagates.

Perhaps the Buddhists have it the easiest. Everyone can have his or her own personal Buddha enshrined in his or her home, for daily consultation. I guess this could also apply to people who have a crucifix over their bed. However, I would think that such omnipresence of the Deity could be a bit daunting because one would feel that Divine judgment is taking place every moment of the day; and if not that, at least it would keep a person on his or her toes.

In Judaism, which is naturally my particular interest, we do have direct access to God, but the route to God is a collective one. We Jews pray in the plural. The few times that we do worship in the singular, we do not ask for selfish considerations, but rather seek something for the community. There is power in such "collective bargaining," increasing the chances of an audience with the Almighty, which is far preferable to an audience with any of God's servants, including an audience with the Pope. There is strength in numbers. God might be more apt to listen to a unified voice of the laity, than the lonely cry of the cleric.

Why Pray to God?

Son: Dad, I don't get it. Why do you go to synagogue? You are a committed atheist.

Father: Son, you see Garfinkel sitting over there. He goes to synagogue to talk to God. I go to synagogue to talk to Garfinkel!

It is said that there are no atheists in foxholes. I know this to be true. During the Lebanon War of 1982, I was with my Israeli army unit just north of the Beirut-Damascus Highway, when a hail of Syrian missiles rained down on our outpost. Quickly, we dashed for the bunkers that we had dug around our encampment. Suddenly, I heard an avowed non-believer next to me involuntarily "praying his guts out." Is there anyone who does not do the same when experiencing the slightest bit of turbulence when he or she is 30,000 feet in the air?

Meyer Levin, in his book, *The Harvest*, describes a scene where the deeply religious patriarch of a large and dispersed family gathers his entire clan together in his house at the end of World War I. His children, all having been raised during the Ottoman rule in Palestine, had each adopted a different life style: One became a businessman, an other an Orthodox scholar, and a third a socialist, who helped to found the kibbutz movement. His socialist (and nonbelieving) son had been conscripted into the Turkish army to fight the British. Attempting to escape, he was captured and sent to a prison in Damascus. It had been assumed that he was killed by the Turkish forces. As the family celebrates its reunion after years of dispersion because of the war, the father walks out to the field, deeply saddened that his first-born child is not there. Suddenly, he sees his son approach from the distance. The two men fall into each other's arms. Neither can find the words to express the tumultuous emotion of the moment, until simultaneously and intuitively they recite together, despite the theological worlds that separate them, the traditional Jewish prayer for a safe journey.

In the fight against evil, according to tradition, a Jew relies upon three weapons, which occupy a central place in the High Holiday liturgy: "Repentance, prayer and charity can avert the evil decree." Of these three, prayer, once the strongest in the arsenal of Judaism, has become the weakest. Prayer used to be the answer to every problem, but today it is the problem itself. Is prayer obsolete? Are we really missing anything important in our spiritual and moral development if we do not pray? Is there any value to prayer for the modern man and woman? Is prayer an exercise in futility? Most important of all: Does God really hear our prayers? If so, what does He or She do with our supplications? How do we discern an answer?

Part of the reason we feel that prayer does not serve our purpose is because whenever we attempt to pray, particularly from a prayer book or within the confines of a formal service, we are left with a feeling that it is as dry as dust, that what we are experiencing is a tedious mumbling of words. What should we expect, an instant rush? Was it ever claimed that religious feeling could come easily like water from a faucet? What worthwhile intellectual or spiritual goal can be reached without an investment of time and energy? In everything that we do, steadfastness and intimacy are the prerequisites for proficiency. Such is the case with prayer. It is hard work to pray. So, what are the advantages of making this effort?

Prayer serves as a means to safeguard memory. Karl Marx (1818 — 1883), the German social philosopher and chief modern theorist of socialism and communism, gave atheists one of their strongest arguments: "Religion is the opium of the masses. It is an escape, a way of forgetting reality." I wonder which religion he had in mind. Jews always prayed, not to forget, but to remember.

Jews are a people of memory. Every ritual, every occasion is tied up with a recollection of an event of joy or sorrow. Jewish holidays are a collective memory. Bitter herbs on *Passover*[1] reminds Jews of their ancestors' enslavement in ancient Egypt. To forget this would mean the loss of what should be the most tender spot in the Jewish heart — empathy for the downtrodden, a passion for freedom. The *Chanukah*[2] *Menorah*[3] speaks of the courage and self-sacrifice of enduring generations of Jews. The Sabbath candles revive the mystery of the Creation. And when Jews stand up to say the *Kaddish*, they remember those they loved.

The Baal Shem Tov said: "Remembrance is the root of redemption." This is a profound thought if one bears in mind the utter confusion of the amnesia victim. A person without a memory becomes helpless. Failing to remember the past, we are doomed to repeat it. There is no culture, no progress and no redemption from

---

1. The Jewish holiday that celebrates the Israelites' escape from Egyptian bondage. The name for *Passover* derives from the biblical passage: "For that night I [God] will go through the land of Egypt and strike down every first-born in the land of Egypt, both man and beast; and I will mete out punishments to all gods in Egypt, I, the Lord. And the blood on the houses in which you dwell shall be a sign for you: When I see the blood, I will **pass over** you, so that no plague will destroy you when I strike the land of Egypt" (*Exodus* 12:12-13).

2. "Dedication" in Hebrew, *Chanukah* is the festival commemorating the rededication of the Holy Temple by the Maccabees in 165 B.C.E., three years after it was desecrated by the Syrian king, Antiochus.

3. A candelabrum, the *Menorah* was originally made by the artist Bezalel, in the Sinai wilderness and placed in the Tabernacle (*Exodus* 25:31-40; 31:1-6).

the evils of yesterday if we do not remember. Another name for the Jewish High Holidays is the "Days of Remembrance." A section of the prayers is called "Remembrances." In particular, it is at the *Yizkor* ("Let one remember") service — the memorial service — when one recalls those who have died. These prayers become deeply imprinted within the Jew, within very private thoughts. At that time, Jews remember those who used to sit next to them, the familiar face of a mother or a father, the closeness or rivalries of a brother or a sister, the affection of, or arguments with, a friend. Sometimes recollections mingle with feelings of remorse and guilt for things left undone or unsaid, haunting memories that may even bring shame.

Are there any memories without some regrets? Inevitably the hour of prayer turns into an inventory of conscience. And so, prayer not only serves as a key to memory, but also as a door to promoting self-judgment and self-improvement. This reminds me of a parable of a sensitive young architect, who, at the sight of an ugly structure, would suffer physical pain verging on apoplexy. One day he took a walk in his neighborhood and saw a new house. Its ugliness nearly made him faint. He was so afraid that he might see the house again, that he took the only sure way of avoiding the sight of it — he moved into it himself. Then the house became so familiar to him that he never really saw it again, and lived happily ever after. I suspect that this can be the case with any one of us. We become so adjusted to who we are that we come to accept ourselves uncritically. Perhaps this is the most significant benefit of prayer. The confessional element is never absent from worship. Prayer offers one the opportunity to examine oneself.

While this sounds all well and good, I am still plagued. Is this the ultimate aim of prayer? The purification, enlightenment and uplifting of one's inner self? Community and introspection are a means to an end, not an end in and of themselves. And, that end is to reach God on some communicative plane, which is done in a communal setting — a by-product of synagogual prayer. There is power in numbers. After all, all prayers are directed toward God, as one thanks, praises and petitions Him or Her.

My question is: Where is God in this whole process? If we use prayer only as a means to address issues of remembrance, loneliness, alienation, guilt, self-examination, then it could very well be that God is not part of the worship process. If that is the case, why direct our prayers to God? Because that is how the prayer book is designed? If we can never be sure that God can "deliver the goods," or the opposite of what we pray for happens, then what do we do?

There are so many things I am praying for in these final hours. Needless to say, I am disappointed, and so is my family. However, I also know that even though the die is cast, and there is nothing more that can be done to save me, the deep-seated emotional need to pray never ceases. It seems so natural to pray, so ingrained to plead with God to spare us from a certain fate. I am slowly discovering that true worship may not be a petition to God at all, but rather a sermon to oneself, a conversation with God, not unlike the one I am having right now. It is a search for comfort, which all of us so desperately need.

Does God Need So Much Praise?

What's with this incessant praise that we heap upon God? If anyone lavished such adulation upon me, I would be walking on air. What can God be possibly thinking when He or She hears such rapturous reverence in the weekday morning service:

> Therefore, we are obliged to **thank You, praise You, glorify, bless, sanctify, and offer praise and thanks to Your Name.**

Understandably, such bountiful adoration does not grow out of a vacuum. It is all predicated on our appreciation of all the great gifts that God has bestowed upon us — the greatest of all being the gift of life itself.

But, what about all those things that go wrong — all those tragedies, human and natural, that tear us asunder? Do we just continue to heap praise upon God no matter what happens around us? Even if we are genuinely grateful for so much good in our lives, does God really need all those generous and indulgent *Psalms* of praise uttered every morning, culminating in an orgy of unabashed adoration that seemingly has no limits — the *Kaddish*, recited countless times every day:

> May God's great Name grow exalted and sanctified in the world that God created and willed. May God give reign to His/Her

Rulership in your lifetimes and in your days, and the lifetimes of
the entire family of Israel, swiftly and soon. Now respond: Amen.
May God's great Name be blessed forever and ever.
**Blessed, praised, glorified, dignified, extolled, mighty, lofty,
and lauded be the Name of the Holy One, Blessed is God**
[Blessed is God] **beyond any blessing and song, praise and
consolation that are uttered in the world.** [Now respond: Amen].

What is so amazing about this prayer of boundless praise is that it is
also said when one is in mourning, when basically one's primal
reaction is to devaluate God, not raise Him or Her on a pedestal of
Heavenly adjectives. Go figure!

Is God embarrassed by such sycophantic fawning? I can just
hear the Almighty saying: "Hello... Get a life!" It is almost
unimaginable that anyone could tolerate such hyperbole. I would
think that after a while God would begin to doubt the sincerity of
such flattery, especially if there is a sense that what the worshipper
is really trying to do is to court a Divine favor. Indeed, such obsequi-
ousness must hide an ulterior motive: the petitionary element of
prayer, whereby we ask God for something.

In the *Talmud*, a Jew is instructed: "You should not over praise
the Almighty" (*Megillah* 18a). Why? Because such hyperbolic
praise could mean that the worshippers really have: "high praises in
their throats and two-edged swords in their hand" (*Psalms* 149:6).
The Psalmist is very insightful. Exaggerated thanks to God can
seem disingenuous. My suspicion is that many people who inflate
their praise for the Almighty do so in the hope that God will
overlook something that they have done that deserves Divine
condemnation.

It strikes one that these incessant compliments meted out to
God by parishioners, who obviously are true believers despite the
"God-awful" things that happen in our world, may be no more than
idol-worship. If one is commanded to "walk humbly with Your
God" (*Micah* 6:8), then one would expect humility to be a Holy

attribute. So, why do believers insist on massaging God's ego? Whose need is greater? Ours to praise God or God's to receive our praise? Moreover, why should people believe in a God who seeks such flattery?

I have not kept score, establishing a Chinese menu of an "A" column of those events for which God really merits praise and a "B" column of those occurrences for which God really merits scrutiny. Indeed, some natural tragedies are so horrendous in the magnitude of suffering they cause that they defy human understanding. It seems they leave no reason to justify even the smallest amount of Heavenly praise.

I am stuck. I want to give praise when praise is due, but like everyone else, I cannot help assessing blame when things go wrong. Since it should matter little to God whether we praise, thank or blame Him or Her, then my suggestion is to treat matters consigned to God's area of responsibility in the same evaluative manner as we apply our judgment to fellow human beings. We should acknowledge the things we do that are praiseworthy, while at the same time we recognize those actions that are blameworthy.

Is There Divine Retribution (Reward and Punishment)?

Surely, God takes into account a balance of payments; that is, subtracting one's shortcomings from one's achievements. My arithmetic indicates that I have more in the credit column than in the debit column. I am trying to be objective here, for that is what I have been told by everyone, not just my family.

This leads to a serious discussion of reward and punishment. Is there really such a concept in the Divine realm? In earthly matters, while it does not always play itself out fairly, there is a pretty well-defined system, if not of reward and punishment, then of cause and effect. Certain behaviors on our part result in certain consequences. However, the formula is not so neat. Doing well on a job does not always guarantee advancement. An objectively inferior worker might be promoted ahead of someone else because of family connections. But, for the most part, the person who works hard is rewarded accordingly.

We educate our children by the tried and true "behavior modification" of reward and punishment. Powerful nations do the same with satellite countries, employing the diplomatic "carrot and stick." Then again, Neville Chamberlain's policy of appeasement toward Adolf Hitler after Germany's takeover of Czechoslovakia had far-reaching and devastating consequences for the entire world.

Truth and consequences (often dire) are simply part of the interaction process, whereby we either keep friends or lose them. Causality is not only a factor in human relations, but also a part of the physical sciences. The entire notion of experimentation is based on cause and effect. Experimentation with different serums resulted in a vaccine that prevents polio.

Beyond the world of laboratory research, which is often beyond our comprehension, is the world that we all know, that we encounter daily — the world of natural wonders and natural disasters. An oil spill in the ocean causes the deaths of many creatures living in the sea. Months of bristling sun and no rain produce a drought and its frequent derivative, famine. A steady rainfall results in plush landscapes, plentiful food and awe-inspiring rainbows (or perhaps devastating floods and typhoons).

All the above indicates that we understand the relationship between cause and effect, reward and punishment. Yet, it seems almost impossible to apply that understanding to behaviors that would seem Divinely inspired. At what point does God punish us for behaviors that would be considered Divinely abusive? Or, is there no connection? We know that the Hebrew song *Yigdal* (God will be great) that often concludes religious services, and reads, "God metes out reward exactly according to one's good work, and punishes one exactly according to one's crime," cannot possibly be true. For example, Ethel and Julius Rosenberg, the convicted communist spies of the Fifties, received the dealth penalty. Their conviction and subsequent capital punishment has aroused controversy that is still debated today. Who is to say that their punishment fit their crime? It is important to note that their fate was determined by a judicial system heavily influenced by the temper of the times, the McCarthy period, which perpetuated the "red" communist scare when the United States was locked in the

Cold War with the former Soviet Union. Today, a communist spy would not be sent to the electric chair.

So, who computes in fair measure the punishment for wrongdoings? The appointed legal guardians of the judicial system? Are they like the prophets of old, God's servants? More so, is a jury of twelve men and women God's administering angels? Is a Divine system of reward and punishment dependent on human implementation? Is it subject to variations based on specific historical time-frames? We have all been taught that God possesses an "eternal now," that His or Her actions are immutable, universal, absolute and everlasting.

> I believe with complete faith that the Creator, Blessed be His Name, is unique, and there is no uniqueness like His in any way, and that He alone is our **God, Who was, Who is and Who always will be** (Maimonides' *Thirteen Articles of Faith*).

If so, it would defy all logic that God would change His or Her mind based on circumstances. More so, it would make little sense for God to entrust the conduct of Divine judgment to us mortals, who are by our very nature mercurial, subject to persuasion, coercion and compromise. Truth either is or is not. It cannot be reduced to relativism. The Christian Bible, the Hebrew Scriptures and the Islamic *Koran* all emphasize that God is a God of Truth, *Emet* in Hebrew and *Al-Haq* in Arabic. As far as these three monotheistic religions are concerned, truth is absolute. Therefore, on a Divine level, the concept of reward and punishment is problematic.

For someone like myself, who feels that he and his family are being short-changed by my early death, how can we ever know if this is a punishment for a transgression I may have committed, and of which I remain totally unaware? Unfortunately, I do not have the leisure time to examine my actions so as to see if I deserve an early demise. If there is any truth to the view that the older one gets the better one's long-term memory becomes, then as far as I can surmise, based on what I can remember of my past, God has given me and my family the raw end of the "reward and punishment" deal. I might add that, at my relatively young age, I could still have contributed much to the betterment of society, as I tried to do in the past.

Clearly, a mistake was made. Sadly, or rather tragically, this mistake is fatal. You would think that God could correct such a terminal error, but either He or She chooses not to, or simply cannot, because it is obvious that I am one of millions of such Celestial slip-ups that occur daily. For God to deal with all the injustices in the world, all of His or Her time would be spent on correcting these Heavenly blunders. Given such thoughts, I must conclude that, in order for God to remain perfect, He or She has nothing to do with my imminent death. Does it follow then that God had little to do with my life as well? This seems to be the logical conclusion that I can draw from my lethal ordeal, which is not very comforting.

It would seem that Divine retribution, one of the philosophical pillars of any theology, is a concept that defies definition and application. If it cannot be designated or related, then one of the cards in the Divine deck is seriously flawed. I may be getting ahead of myself, because I should really save the end of my days for the end of my treatise. The quintessential question, can we know fully what our mortality is all about and how it relates to all the concomitant issues related to finitude, will have to be dealt with much later on in my search for some Divine logic to my life.

Does God Grant Free Will?

Perhaps God is simply not part of our earthly existence. And that is how God determined the order of things to be. It is not we who do not allow God to enter our world, it is God, out of respect for the human spirit of His or Her creatures, who chooses to let free will rule our lives — for good and for bad.

We have now arrived at a discussion of Free Will versus Determinism, a reasonable discussion to conduct after having just raised the subject of reward and punishment. As much as we all cherish our freedom, taken to its extreme, unmeasured and limitless freedom can result in tragedies of unfathomable proportions. For example, is there any Jew (or any person of goodwill) who would not have readily forfeited a little of his or her free will, if not all, for some Divine intervention during the time of the Holocaust. I can imagine that many a person would have willingly sacrificed his or her autonomy to have had God put a stop to the Black Plague. A little Heavenly intercession might have turned the Dark Age into a more tolerable "Dim Age." I guess I am arguing for a little compromise on both sides: We give up some of our free will and God gets a little more involved in the events of the day. The reason we should seek compromise is because too much Divine intrusion can wreak havoc, as was the case with the Crusades, which allegedly were waged in the name of God. Of course, if God is Good, then either His or Her involvement was an aberration; or those who claimed that they were carrying out God's Will simply misled us.

It can be a slippery slope. How would we envision God interceding on our behalf? More significantly, what type of event would determine Divine intervention? Might God let the genocide of the Armenians at the turn of the twentieth century slide by, and yet halt the genocide of European Jews some decades later? Just as we are often confronted with excruciating choices, where we are damned if we do and damned if we don't, it would seem that God faces similar dilemmas in making the critical choice of when to say: "Enough is enough"!

However, on closer examination, the very notion of free will runs contrary to religious tradition. The Old and New Testaments are filled with Divine direction, as is the *Koran*. God's guiding hand is felt in virtually every chapter and verse of these three texts, holy to different religions. In these sacred books, rare is the heroic character who does not claim to act or speak in the name of God. Some dominant personalities who pretend to speak in God's name are dealt with harshly, as was the case with Korach, who tried to lead a rebellion against Moses, and found himself, by Divine decree, swallowed up by the earth (*Numbers* 16:1-35). Did such a punishment fit the crime?

According to the written word, the ancient history of Christianity, Judaism and Islam is a dramatic accounting of God's intimate involvement in the lives of the people of those times. Divine intervention was visibly experienced and clearly documented. Yet, since the time of the Old Testament prophet Malachi, since the close of the early Christian era as recorded in the New Testament, and since the last *Sura* of the *Koran* was written, it has been difficult, if not impossible, to see or feel Divine historical engagement. Any clouds that hover over us are generally considered to be a forewarning of an impending storm, not a sign that God is about to perform some supernatural act to "save the day," although the peculiarities of such natural wonders most certainly arouse within us extraterrestrial bewilderment. A bolt of lightning or a clap of thunder does not necessarily indicate a series of tragic events, any more than does a rainbow signify the dawn of universal enlightenment, tolerance and peace.

Is it all or nothing, that is, can there be no compromise between Free Will and Determinism? Are these two schools of thought mutually exclusive? There is no such thing as being a little pregnant; and likewise, it would seem that there can be no application of a judicious amount of Free Will or a modest use of Determinism. Conceding some of the purity of either end of the spectrum just doesn't work.

In human interactions, we will always find ourselves limited. No one is totally free to do as he or she wishes. Forces beyond our control limit our actions. I am free to think as I wish, but that does not mean I am free to realize all my desires. So, let us now examine this tension between Free Will and Determinism more fully.

Can Philosophy Settle the Conflict between Free Will and Determinism?

I have hinted that theologians and philosophers are often of little help to us plebeians. Their intellect is far beyond the comprehension of the average person who seeks more simplified and direct answers to questions surrounding God's existence, or at least answers that are readily understandable. However, despite my skepticism and because the discourse on Determinism versus Free Will is critical to understanding our relationship with and/or belief in God, I thought it would be wise to go beyond my own musings on this difficult subject, and turn to some of the great intellectuals who have carved out their philosophical immortality in dealing with these metaphysical concerns. (Personally, I am more interested in physical immortality than philosophical immortality.) The accepted assumption is that they would be of great help. But, let us see if we can make heads or tails out of the following theses on Free Will versus Determinism.

The belief that our actions are the result of antecedent causes has been formulated naturalistically and theistically. The naturalistic view sees human beings as part of the machinery of the universe. In such a world, every event is caused by preceding events, which in turn are caused by still earlier events, *ad infinitum*.

Since we are a part of this causal chain, our actions are also determined by antecedent causes. In this view, no human action could have been performed otherwise than it was in fact performed. Thus, according to Determinism, my taking a pleasurable snooze in the middle of the afternoon, lying luxuriously on my comfortable couch, rather than taking a power-nap sitting upright in my rocking chair, is not a free choice, but entirely brought about by previous factors.

The theistic view, however, holds that all events, including behavior, are caused (determined) by God. Therefore, the concept of Free-Will or Self-Determinism contradicts the sovereignty of God. If God is truly in control of all things, then no one could act contrary to God's Will, which is what Self-Determinism must maintain. Hence, for God to be sovereign, He or She must cause every event, be it human or otherwise. Our will could never act unless God moved it. Thus, to speak of human acts as self-caused would be like speaking of nothing causing something. Therefore, the thesis that freedom is given in accordance with God's Will and not our will seems to be consistent with the most basic understanding of God's role in our lives.

To make this whole duality of thought — Free Will versus Determinism — more complicated, I will now turn to the German philosopher, Immanuel Kant (1724-1804), who was the first philosopher to draw attention to the dilemma between the two. Kant formulated his views in support of deterministic philosophy, as espoused in his two major works: *Critique of Pure Reason* and *Critique of Practical Reason.* I will quote an excerpt from each to see if what Kant writes is of any help.

From the *Critique of Pure Reason*:

> Every human being has an empirical character for his power of choice, which is nothing other than a certain causality of his

reason... This empirical character must be drawn from appearances as effect, and from the rule which experience provides, all the actions of the human being in appearance are determined in accord with the order of nature by his empirical character and the other cooperating causes; and if we could investigate all the appearances of his power of choice down to their basis, then there would be no human action that we could not predict with certainty, and recognize as necessary given its preceding conditions. Thus in regard to this empirical character there is no freedom, and according to this character we can consider the human being solely by observing, and, as happens in anthropology, by trying to investigate the moving causes of his actions physiologically.

Now, if that does not clear matters up, let us turn to the *Critique of Practical Reason*:

The concept of causality as natural necessity, as distinguished from the concept of causality as freedom, concerns only the existence of things insofar as it is determinable in time and hence as appearances, as opposed to their causality as things in themselves. Indeed, even if I assume that my whole existence is independent from any alien cause (such as God), so that the determining grounds of my causality and even of my whole existence are not outside me, this would not in the least transform that natural necessity into freedom... If, then, one wants to attribute freedom to a Being whose existence is determined in time, one cannot, so far at least, except this Being from the law of natural necessity as to all events in its existence and consequently as to its actions as well; for that would be tantamount to handing it over to blind chance. But since this law unavoidably concerns all causality of things so far as their existence in time is determinable, if this were the way in which one had to represent also the existence of these things-in-themselves, then freedom would have to be rejected as a null and impossible concept.

Whew! I am glad that we straightened that out. But, what about the argument for Free Will? Here we could turn to Thomas Hobbes (1588-1679) or David Hume (1711-1776), the two best-known advocates of this position, but I am not sure that quoting them in support of the philosophical argument for Free Will would be any more edifying than what Immanuel Kant explained.

One of the most eminent and studied philosophers who attempted to explain the compatibility between Determinism and Free Will was Rene Descartes, the French rationalist (1596-1650), who was the father of philosophical dualism, in which mind and matter operate in a coordinated fashion. But, I will forego discussing his philosophy as well, so as not to confuse the reader any more than I already have. Indeed, one more ride on this philosophical roller coaster would be far too dizzying. It is time to stop "putting Des-**cart**-es before the horse," that is, placing heavy philosophical discussions before good old common sense, because such an approach only confuses matters.

Three times a day during the week (with the exception of the Sabbath and certain holidays), a Jew offers up the same thirteen benedictions to God. The first of these petitionary prayers is titled — *Bina* (Understanding):

> You favor Adam [the generic human being] with knowledge, and teach understanding to mortals. May you continue to favor us with knowledge, understanding and **insight**. Blessed is the Lord, giver of knowledge.

The Hebrew word for "insight" is *heskeil*, which has as its root the word *sechel* (common sense). First knowledge is given, and then understanding — necessary intellectual tools. One can be a great intellect — philosopher — filled with knowledge and understanding, but without the additive of insight and common sense, a person will never be able to decipher his or her role in the world, and purpose for being.

We are much better off if we address the issue of Free Choice or the lack thereof in simpler terms than offered by these acknowledged great thinkers. In order to feel a little better about ourselves, I will quote the Nobel Laureate in Physics, Albert Einstein (1879-1955): "Honestly, I cannot understand what people mean when they talk about freedom of the human will." If Einstein could not understand this discourse, then who are we to feel badly that any discussion of Determinism and Free Will baffles us? If such a genius as Einstein essentially tells us through his Theory of Relativity that everything is connected to what came before, who are we lesser peons to think otherwise?

In his song, *The Ballad In Plain D*, popular folk-philosopher Bob Dylan sings a tragic tale of his attempt to "steal away" a younger sister from a "mother an' (older) sister." Like a true Determinist, Dylan writes that the outcome of his ordeal was foreseen, for not only is no one free from the consequences of his or her actions, not even "are birds free from the chains of the skyway":

Of the two sisters, I loved the young.
With sensitive instincts, she was the creative one.
The constant scapegoat, she was easily undone
By the jealousy of others around her...
An' so it did happen like it could've been foreseen,
The timeless explosion of fantasy's dream.
At the peak of the night, the king an' the queen
Tumbled all down to pieces.
"The tragic figure," her sister did shout,
"Leave her alone, goddamn you, get out."
An' I in my armor, turnin' about

An' nailin' her in the ruins of her pettiness.
Beneath a bare lightbulb, the plaster did pound.
Her sister an' I in a screamin' battleground.
An' she in between, the victim of sound

Soon shattered as a child to the shadows.
All is gone, all is gone, admit it, take flight.
I gagged in contradiction, tears blindin' my sight.
My mind it was mangled, I ran into the night,
Leavin' all of love's ashes behind me.

Ah, my friends from the prison, they ask onto me:
"How good, how good does it feel to be free"?
An' I answer them most mysteriously:
"Are birds free from the chains of the skyway"?

In short, these immense minds, from the logical Kant and the deductive Descartes to the brilliant Einstein and the poetic Dylan, only help us slightly to deal with the questions that opened up our topic of Free Will versus Determinism, questions that have to do with the "three Big Os" — Divine omnipotence, omniscience and omnipresence: If there is such a thing as Free Will, would we be willing to compromise it in order to prevent a tragedy of the magnitude of the Holocaust? How would we envision God interceding on our behalf? More significantly, what type of event would determine Divine intervention; and how would we recognize Heavenly influence? Can we? On the other hand, if there is no Free Will, if God dictates all, then what purpose do we serve? To feed some Divine ego? How selfish can God be?

Are We God's Puppets?

It is quite obvious that most people who define themselves as religious, believe that God is intimately involved in the history and destiny of their respective religions. Indeed, the entire biblical narrative, both the Old and New Testaments, portrays God as pulling the strings of virtually all historical and personal events. As discussed earlier, the $64,000 question is: Do Moslems, Jews and Christians believe in the same God? If God is One, then He or She is the One God of all. And, if so, why do Protestants and Catholics wage war against each other, as do Jews and Moslems? The belief recorded in these three sacred books is that God is in control of all that happens in the universe, and this overarching power is given daily expression in each religion's liturgical texts. Liturgy is the codification of "inspired" formulations whereby an individual can pray to God.

If each belief-system purports a theology that God is intimately involved in a particular religion, how can any sane person accept a God who allows unspeakable cruelty to enter the world? If theistic determinism is correct, are we to unconditionally accept starvation in Biafra or genocide in Bosnia or Sudan? If God determines everything that happens, should He or She not stand trial for war crimes? Or, could it just be possible that God is not involved in the historical development of our own religious traditions? Does having the freedom to make decisions necessarily invalidate a belief in a Higher Being? Or, if we are limited in our choices, or our decisions are predetermined because of the natural order of things, is God even a necessity in our lives?

My problem is that if everything is preordained, theistically, not naturally, then what was the use of my becoming actively involved in events of the day in the hope of altering their course? What good did having a social conscience do for me, if everything was fated to turn out a certain way, irrespective of my good intentions and noble actions? If this is the case, I rather fancy my life as having been pretty useless — a depressing thought. I may have wasted my time being so terribly concerned about the poor, the disenfranchised, the persecuted. These people were destined to suffer their lot in life. Had I only realized that, I could have led a much more hedonistic life, and had a lot more fun along the way. Then again, in the natural world, it is entirely possible that we are part of the process of cause and effect; that is, certain behaviors on our part set in motion a chain reaction of events for which we are responsible.

The confrontation between Determinism and Free Will becomes more pronounced when placed in a Divine context. All of us accept that none of us is completely free to do as we please, and that there is a relationship between cause and effect. We do not really need Kant or Hobbes or Descartes to tell us that. But, the ready acceptance of the relationship between behavior/actions and their concomitant consequences is not easily transferable to God's realm. Here we are caught in the middle between two polar views, which cannot be harmonized. Either God is intimately involved in history or is not. Both possibilities sow confusion. Certainly, as this polarity of thought relates to prayer, we would ask: If one believes in the efficacy of prayer, and God is the object of worship, how can someone pray to a God who allows so much cruelty to be inflicted upon His or Her creatures? If, on the other hand, one believes that

God is not intimately involved in history, why bother to pray to the Almighty?

We are all familiar with the story of the Israelites' enslavement in Egypt and their eventual escape to freedom through Divine intervention, which God demonstrated by the parting of the Red Sea. This miraculous event-to-be was already revealed to Abraham, who preceded the entire exodus story by five hundred years.

> When the sun went down, Abram [Abraham's original name] fell into a deep sleep; and lo, a horror of great darkness overcame him. And God said to Abram: "Know for certain that your offspring will be strangers in a land that is not theirs, and they will serve masters who will torture them for four hundred years. But, that nation [and its masters], to which they will be as slaves, I will judge [harshly]; and afterwards, they will go free … and you shall go to your fathers in peace; and be buried at a ripe-old age" (*Genesis* 15:12-15).

What better example can there be of God being intimately involved in, and in control of, the collective history and destiny of a people? But, the question is: Why? Why did God set it up this way? What could be the possible reason for sending an entire people into enslavement for so many years, only to then set them free? Are we to understand from this narrative that one is only entitled to redemption after one suffers? Is it God's design that happiness should only be experienced after a lengthy period of abject misery? Are we to believe that the only way the Jews could have achieved independence after two thousand years of statelessness was to first have six million of them murdered?

This is a good segue to the notion of collective punishment. I have always felt that collective punishment is immoral. It is true that one person's behavior can adversely affect the behavior of others. How often has a teacher held an entire class responsible for the ill-behavior of a few? In order to get to the bottom of some sort of dastardly act in the classroom, such as a few children taunting one particular kid who is socially inept or physically awkward, often a teacher will threaten to punish the entire class if those who actually tortured the boy or girl do not come forward and confess. On the one hand, we tell our children not to give in to peer pressure; on the other hand, we use peer pressure to control behavior.

Army discipline operates on collectivity. A soldier messes up, and his or her comrades suffer the consequences. This method is also employed to prevent covering up for others or breaking that unwritten macho "code of silence." Then there is the sergeant who stands in front of his soldiers, barking: "Who is responsible for this"? And, all the soldiers step forward and say: "I am, sir"!

The first literary discussion of collective punishment appears in the Bible, with the dramatic story of the evil behavior of the people of Sodom and Gomorrah as described in the eighteenth and nineteenth chapters of *Genesis*. Here we see Abraham arguing with God against destroying both cities and all their inhabitants, with his famous plea before the Almighty:

> Will You destroy the innocent along with the guilty? What if there should be fifty innocent within the city; will You then wipe out the place and not forgive it for the sake of the innocent fifty who are in it? Far be it from You to do such a thing, to bring death upon the innocent as well as upon the guilty, so that the innocent and guilty fare alike. Far be it from You! Shall not the Judge of all earth deal justly (18:23-25)?

Why would Abraham even challenge God? Does he doubt God's intentions? God agrees not to destroy the two cities, if Abraham can produce only ten innocent people. We know how the story ends, with God raining down on Sodom and Gomorrah a sulfurous fire that annihilates the cities, their inhabitants and all vegetation. Are we to believe that there was not one innocent individual in either of the cities?

Is God trying to set up a "straw man"? Once again, if we are to learn from God, using Him or Her as the most significant Being for us to imitate, then who can blame nations, particularly the Jewish people in Israel, God's supposedly "chosen people," for carrying out acts of collective punishment against their enemies — in Israel's case, against Palestinian suicide bombers, by destroying the homes of these murderers' families? Are we to surmise from this story that collective forms of punishment are the only definitive way to deal with evil? When nations wage war, frequently an entire village can be destroyed, because within it are a few rebel fighters. Such was the case during the U.S. involvement in the Vietnam War. Are we commanded "to bring death upon the innocent as well as upon the guilty, so that the innocent and guilty fare alike"?

Could it be that the reason the global fight against terrorism has not succeeded is because it has been waged half-heartedly? Instead of just overthrowing the Taliban in Afghanistan, perhaps the United States should have simply wiped the country off the face of the map, as God did with Sodom and Gomorrah. What of Hiroshima and Nagasaki. Nuking them seems like child's play compared to some of the actions carried out by God. Then again, maybe destroying Dresden in World War II was the only means to bring the Nazis to their heels, for what better example in modern times of Sodom and Gomorrah is there than Nazi Germany?

None of us wants to believe that God is responsible for natural catastrophes and historical tragedies. However, to exclude God from any role in the natural and human order of events is also a difficult notion to accept, and runs contrary to the most basic understanding of religiously recorded history. Yet, if God is in total control, if God knows what the end holds for us, then what would motivate us to do anything? Either things will work out for the good — or not. If we are merely puppets being pulled by some Heavenly strings, does that mean we are all essentially "dummies"?

The story that illustrates this dilemma best is the biblical account of God telling Abraham to sacrifice his son Isaac. The narrative is uniquely significant because Abraham is considered the common father of Judaism and Islam. (The place where the fabled sacrifice allegedly took place is Mount Moriah in Jerusalem, which is sacred ground to the Jews and which is situated today in the middle of the Dome of the Rock, a holy shrine to Moslems.)

> God put Abraham to the test, saying to him, "Abraham," and he answered, "Here I am." And God continued, "Take your son, your favored one, Isaac, whom you love, and go to the land of Moriah, and offer him there as a burnt-offering on one of the heights, which I will point out to you..." They arrived [Abraham and Isaac] at the place of which God had told them. Abraham built an altar there; he laid out the wood; he bound his son Isaac; he laid him on the altar, on top of the wood. And Abraham picked up the knife to slay his son. Then an angel of the Lord cried out to him from the heaven: "Abraham! Abraham"! And Abraham answered, "Here I am." And the angel said, "Do not raise your hand against the boy, or do anything to him. For now I [God] know that you fear Me, since you have not withheld your son, your favored one from Me" (*Genesis* 22:1-2, 9-12).

As one might imagine, this story has prompted countless commentaries and numerous books. If, according to the Jewish tradition, Abraham is considered to be its first monotheist, given God's demand of the very first believer in the singularity of God, what, in God's name, is going on here? This seems like a pretty warped way to show appreciation for that person (Abraham) who popularized for the world the concept of one God; although, here I admit to some confusion, for the notion of child sacrifice is associated with paganism, which contradicts orthodox understandings of Abraham as having a true one-on-one relationship with God.

At first glance, it strikes the casual reader of this story as if God and Abraham are either in complete cahoots with one another, or they are both "off the wall." In either case, there is no narrative in the entire Bible more disturbing than this one. Abraham is commanded by God to kill his own son with a knife in order to prove his ultimate faith in a Higher Being. With such seeming Divine sadism at play, is it any wonder that one might have some problem with belief in God? If this is the manner in which God wants to prove His or Her dominance, then who needs such agony in one's life?

There is nothing more painful than losing a child. When we lose a parent, we forfeit our past. When we lose a child, we are deprived of our future. Not only for the living, but also for the dead, our children's continued existence is what sustains us. Perhaps this is why the story is so strange, for such a sacrifice, had it taken place, would have made a mockery out of Abraham's entire life, which had been based on the Divine promise that he would become the father of a great nation: "I will make you a great nation" (*Genesis* 12:2), but, as pointed out earlier, Divine contradictions are nothing new.

Apparently there is some coordinated game being played here. Those who believe that God is omniscient, omnipotent and omnipresent would claim that psychologically there could be no better way to prove one's absolute and ultimate faith in God than by being willing to sacrifice to the Almighty one's own child (in this case, the only child born of Abraham and his wife, Sarah). Then again, if God is indeed all-knowing, all-powerful, and ever-present, it is obvious that this was all a charade — the ending preordained. God is the playwright, director and producer of a gripping drama, with Abraham and Isaac as the lead actors; and we, the audience, are simply being treated to great theater.

If I wanted to give credit to the authors of this story, whether it be God Him- or Herself, or some biblical scribe who set the literary stage for future Steven King novels, then I would simply say this is a great "almost" murder mystery, for in the end, Isaac is spared. Naturally, as part of the suspense, if Isaac were to be killed, I would want to know how God would guarantee the perpetuation of Abraham's lineage through the only son of Abraham and his wife. Perhaps this story is the forerunner of the school of the "theater of the absurd," as indicated in Woody Allen's rendition of the story in his book, *Without Feathers*:

> **Abraham to God**: But dost this not prove I love Thee, that I was willing to sacrifice mine only son on Thy whim?
>
> **God to Abraham**: It proves that some men will follow any order no matter how asinine, as long as it comes from a resonant, well-modulated voice.

If I wanted to consider this tale as an invitation to a theological discourse of our relationship to God, then I must admit that the plot is most compelling. God is testing the limits of our belief and what we are willing to do when given our "marching orders." Abraham had to be under some Godly spell to be so willing to do God's deadly bidding, otherwise how can anyone explain Abraham's willingness to so readily sacrifice his own kid? And, if Abraham was merely a dupe, genuinely having no idea how the episode would turn out, then we have a pretty sadistic God out there Who will stop at nothing to have His or Her people prove not only their belief in the Almighty, but their total allegiance.

Of course, we have always been taught not to carry out an illegal order or a command that runs contrary to our moral conscience or religious belief. (I have always maintained that issues of moral conscience and matters of religious belief take precedence over national loyalties.) Since Abraham failed to protest God's order either on the grounds of illegality, or moral conscience, or religious beliefs, then the only logical conclusion must be that he had no choice. Then again, why did he argue so forcefully in the matter of Sodom and Gomorrah? He had no free will, certainly not as long as God was holding all the determinist cards. Perhaps the story is not at all about morality, but about obedience.

Let us suppose for the moment that Abraham thought about sacrificing Isaac on his own, that no angel approached him, that he was operating under the Hobbesian theory that he possessed total freedom from Divine dictate, and that he was doing this because it was the tribal ritual of the time; and so his desire to kill his son was not theistically motivated, but sociologically and culturally determined. Would we want God to intervene? Given the amount of child sacrifice that occurs every day in our world, as we send our children off to war, wouldn't a little Holy interference be warranted? However, the moment that we ask God to be our *deus ex machina*, we automatically concede our freedom.

If we were to magnify this story, where it was not just one person affected by God's involvement or non-involvement, but nations, would we then be willing to give up some of our freedom for Divine intervention? How can we ever know whether those who support Determinism or those who advocate Free Will are correct? We are caught in the middle, with each philosophical theory bearing its own set of challenges, neither one of them being particularly comforting — unless, of course, we can find some sort of compatibility between the two. There is a mini-battle for control taking place between God, the Determinist, and us, the Free Will "wanna-bes," not unlike the struggle that often takes place between parents and children during the latter's adolescence. But, like the child who outgrows his or her rebellious teenage years and settles on a familial truce for an extended period of time, until becoming a parent him- or herself when the truce becomes permanent as a result, so too should we be able to reach a modicum of acceptance of some of God's peculiar ways. Should we be able to harmonize the seemingly competing forces of Divine control and free choice, we just might successfully build a case for a "limited" and tightly defined belief in God.

If Sin Exists, Original or Otherwise, What is the Process of Atonement?

Any discourse on Free Will and Determinism that is theistically based necessarily leads to a discussion of the role of sin in our lives. According to Christianity's Pauline soteriology — the doctrine of salvation through faith in Jesus as the Christ — all humankind inherits at birth the guilt of Adam who committed the original sin. Whereas Judaism maintains that, if a person sins, he or she is a sinner, Christianity proclaims that, because all people are sinners, they sin.

The British theologian, Rabbi Louis Jacobs, writes:

> Many people, particularly during the last two centuries, were prepared to challenge the proposition that sin is real. They say that the concept of sin is outdated. Man, in their view, never sins.

Welcome to the world of "sociology" (a sort of "environmental determinism"), the modern discipline that has replaced the philosophical discussion of Free Will versus Determinism. Sociology would hold that the bad or sinful person is a victim of circumstances, a product of his or her environment, both familial and societal. A person is not to blame for his or her faults, for the failure to do right, or rather the persistence to do wrong, to commit sinful acts. All the mistakes an individual makes, all the man and woman-made evils by which the face of humanity is blackened, are due to a faulty upbringing, to inadequate training by stupid parents and teachers (the classic role models), to an unsound economy, a bad society, an unfortunate environment or to psychological maladjustment.

Society takes steps to protect itself against such a person's designs, but admits that he or she is no more to blame for what he or she is or does than an individual afflicted with a bodily disease. This sociological view of the world is perhaps best expressed in the satirical song, "Officer Krupke," from the musical *West Side Story*:

> Our mothers are all junkies,
> Our fathers are all drunks,
> Golly, Moses, naturally we're punks.
> Gee, Officer Krupke, we're very upset,
> We never had the love that every child ought to get.
> We ain't no delinquents,
> We're misunderstood.
> Deep down inside us, there is good!

If we are all destined to be sinners because of either the stain of "original sin" or the sociological reality of our lives, then what is the use of engaging in a constant struggle to overcome our inherent inclination to do evil? Or, for that matter, to even combat evil? Or, further, to take any control over our own lives? Can it be that what leads to sin is that human beings can resist anything but temptation? Was that Adam's downfall? The question that must be asked is: Do we accept such a world-view, whereby we are essentially pawns in the hands of another being, either celestial or earthly? What about those who are truly good people, who have fought against evil in their own immediate lives or in a wider milieu?

When I think about the manner in which I conducted myself

over the years, in both my personal and professional life, there is little doubt I had much to improve. There were simply too many acts I carried out, or words that I uttered, which begged for forgiveness. Among my most grievous faults was my premature judgment of people. I overrated very few, and belittled too many. I remember the low opinion I had of several of my rabbinic colleagues at the outset of our careers. I thought they were misfits for the profession. However, some time later, I was forced to revise my opinion of their character and ability. Far from being inept, hypocritical and obnoxious — some of the more generous terms I used to describe them — I learned in the course of time that each had become a highly effective and dedicated rabbi, widely respected and beloved in the community. Believe me, I do not need a court of Divine justice to determine the guilt I feel for having wronged people by intent, neglect, misjudgment or miscalculation. Sadly, it is too late for me to do anything about it.

It is not easy to come to terms with sin. The process entails redressing our wrongdoings and asking for forgiveness, but, from whom should we seek exoneration? The most natural route to take is first to turn to the person we have maligned, and ask for some sort of human exculpation; that is, to have the person accept our apology. By the way, that sappy saying in Erich Segal's novel, *Love Story*, "love means never having to say you're sorry," is pure nonsense. Love is having to say you are sorry on numerous occasions. A transgression directed at a loved one is far more painful than a hurt inflicted on an acquaintance.

We should only seek forgiveness once the transgression we have committed is in our conscious mind, and we feel genuine remorse. Only then can we seriously attempt to minimize our sins in the future. This process is acceptable to all religions — even if the concept of original sin is part of a specific religion's world-view. In December of 1977, Los Angeles Lakers' basketball star, Kermit Washington, punched out the Houston Rockets' Rudy Tamjanovich, ending the latter's playing career, and almost his life. It was only after years of volunteer work with the disadvantaged and disabled, of speaking out against violence, of internalizing his terrible act, that Washington felt he could ask forgiveness from Tamjanovich. His healing process lasted twenty-five years, and only in May of 2002 did he confront Tamjanovich, admitting his sin and seeking forgiveness, which he received.

The need for contrition is best described in the biblical story of Jacob and Esau. In ancient times, the eldest son was entitled to inherit the mantle of leadership from his father, which included the transfer of the birthright and the granting of a special blessing. By means of trickery, Jacob, the younger son, steals from Esau, the older, both the birthright and the blessing (*Genesis* 25:19 — 27:46). Fearful of revenge, Jacob flees his familial surroundings, seeking refuge in the house of Bethuel, his mother's father.

While there, Jacob finds himself serving as little more than a slave for Laban, his mother's brother; and, after seven years chooses Laban's daughter, Rachel, for a wife. He surreptitiously slips into her tent at night, but when he wakes up in the morning, he discovers that he has slept with Leah, the elder daughter. Now, that's as good an example of retribution, Divine or otherwise, as I have ever encountered. Only after another seven years, is his desire to receive Rachel fulfilled, and he then has two wives.

It is clear now that Jacob gets the not so subtle hint that what he did to Esau was a calculated misdeed. And so, he sets off on an adventure to confront Esau and make amends for his wrongdoings. Hence, we read of one of Jacob's revelatory dreams: God's angel-messenger enters into a wrestling match with him. Alas, Jacob proves to be a formidable opponent. Subduing the angel with a half-nelson, he virtually pins the Celestial messenger to the mat, agreeing to let him go on the condition that he bestows on him a Divine blessing — an absolution for his earlier transgressions against Esau. At this point, the angel, after inquiring as to his name, which he obviously must have known, said the following:

> Your name will no longer be Jacob, but Israel, for you have struggled with God and men, and have prevailed (*Genesis* 32:28).

According to the great medieval Jewish commentator, Rashi (Rabbi Shlomo Ben Yitzhak, 1040-1105), the name Israel is based on the Hebrew root word "struggle" (legitimate striving), and the name Jacob is based on the Hebrew root word "cunning." Jacob did battle with his conscience, maturing from a deceitful individual into a responsible and honest individual.

Contrition, which leads to reconciliation, requires a process: An internal struggle to overcome the forces of evil within us that cause us to hurt others. Forgiveness for sins committed does not come without effort. The dream sequences of Jacob define the process a religious person must go through to atone for his or her sins. It is two-fold, involving first an inner search of one's conscience, and second, a confrontation with the person against whom the transgression was committed. This process should satisfy the nonbeliever as well; but, for the believer, climbing the ladder leads him or her to Divine compensation, which is ultimately considered the most meaningful form of absolution.

> He [Jacob] had a dream; a ladder was set in the earth and its top reached into the heaven, and angels of God were ascending and descending on it. And God was standing beside him... (*Genesis* 28:12-13).

As for plea-bargaining with our Maker, that is a different can of worms. Maybe I will digress for a moment, and talk about worms. According to the biblical account of the Creation, human beings were the last of the creatures that God created, which means that the lowly worm arrived on the scene before we did. I only mention this because it is such a humbling thought that a disgusting little creature like a worm was higher on God's priority list than we were. Perhaps God was trying to tell us that a little bit of the worm's physical slime rubbed off on us humans, introducing the concept of "human slime." And, we all know plenty of slimy people who relish in committing sins. Chances are there is a little slime in all of us, thereby making all of God's creatures destined to seek Divine dispensation for their sins — great and small. (A big sin would be murdering; a small sin would be telling the clerk at the ticket booth in Disney World that our sixteen-year old child is really fourteen so that we can receive a child's discount.)

The Catholic Church has developed a creative way to deal with sin — the confessional booth. You walk into the booth, ostensibly to confess your sins to the priest, who is shielded from you. And, what is required of you? Well, after a dialogue on why you should feel badly, you are instructed to recite a few "Hail Marys," and to resolve that you will do better, not to repeat your transgression... until the next confessional. It is like the nicotine addict who quits smoking between cigarettes.

I know that by making such a sweeping generalization, I am being glib — a sinful act *per se*. The confessional process, whereby one bounces off a priest his or her real sins, can lead to a genuine act of remorse, especially if the priest is a sensitive facilitator. But, too often the admission of wrongdoing stops at the confessional booth. Confession is not sufficient. Repair is what is demanded, and that requires effort and process and time, as the biblical parables of Jacob so clearly teach us.

A problem with the normative confessional approach, whereby we ask to be absolved of what we have done wrong by seeking "Divine Absolution," either directly from God or from one of God's interlocutors, is that it is a short-cut to forgiveness, requiring little exertion on our part. It is instant gratification. Feel badly one minute, chant some ancient incantations, and "abra cadabra," you feel good again. If you do not like your car, your job, your house, your spouse — just trade them in for newer models. Use, or rather abuse, God to get a light sentence. It is a subtle way of plea-bargaining. Instantaneous satisfaction is an anesthetic. It numbs us so that, at another point in time, we may not realize that we have done anything particularly sinful. It is like the overuse of antibiotics. If they are taken injudiciously, they eventually lose their effectiveness in battling illness.

Leaning exclusively on God is a facile way to avoid confronting not only the person against whom we have sinned, but also our inner self. Even in the case of Jacob, who spent twenty-one years of his life in sinful limbo before he received absolution, God served only as the facilitator, the arbitrator. It was Jacob who had to face Esau.

If we harken back to "Officer Krupke," we see that society's sins of commission may really be sins of omission, for which we all bear some responsibility. Yet, we must inquire as to why we should have to elaborate and enumerate our sins before God. Doesn't God, the alleged omniscient One, know our sins? Catholicism, which promulgates the concept of original sin, would say, "yes." Protestantism varies in its answer depending on the particular denomination, as there is a wide variety of thought spanning from the Southern Baptists to the Unitarians. Judaism and Islam hold that people sin because, to quote *Ecclesiastes*: "There is no righteous person in the world who always does good and never sins" (7:20). Therefore, all of us, original and acquired sinners, must take the paradigmatic route of Jacob, and direct our apology not toward God, but toward our own personal Esaus.

Before we leave the subject of sin, we must ask the question: Is there a place for avenging sin? Should Esau not have gone after Jacob in vengeful retaliation for what he did to him? The natural inclination of an individual is to seek revenge. We all get a perverse satisfaction when we see the guy in the car who is tailgating us, and then passing us on the right at record speed, stopped by a cop. Of course, our smugness here is warranted, for the guy is certainly a hazard on the roads. Yet, too often thoughts of revenge go beyond balance and reason, as we hope to build ourselves up on the backs of others, or sing our own praises by putting others down.

Often we substitute getting mad with getting even. But, vengeance can be a terrible taskmaster; and, there is no such thing as "sweet revenge." It is amazing how many precious hours we spend harboring grudges and nursing old resentments. It may be said that time is the "great healer," but yesterday's slights are not easily forgotten. In order to overcome resentments, we do not need more time, but more insight, more understanding, more forgiveness, and most importantly, more objectivity.

What of revenge on a national level? Whenever there is a suicide bombing in Israel, the almost immediate reaction is to avenge the deaths of the innocents. Often, the reaction lacks practical and moral consideration. While security concerns warrant a response, one would hope for a balanced one; and that the brutality of the other side will not serve as a common denominator to justify excesses. Is capital punishment, the ultimate form of revenge, Divinely demanded? Unfortunately, the Divine model contains a lot of vengeance; to wit, the biblical verdict for a homosexual, which strikes one as particularly vengeful:

> If a man lies with a man as one lies with a woman, both of them have done what is detestable. They must be put to death; their blood will be on their own heads (*Leviticus* 20:13).

Look at the generation of Noah. Before he had a chance to say: "You wouldn't," God wiped out everything, except two of each species, so that the world could regenerate and repopulate itself. If we have established that there is the notion of collective sin, clearly here God has initiated the concept of collective punishment. This strikes me as quite problematic, particularly since we read:

> You shall not hate your brother in your heart. Rather, you must reason with your kin, so that you do not incur guilt on his account. But, **you must not seek vengeance,** nor bear a grudge against your kin; you shall love your neighbor as yourself — **I am the Lord** (*Leviticus* 19:17-18).

The above quote is from the Holiness Code, which includes a litany of "dos" and "don'ts" that guarantee human beings to live together honorably and respectfully. Within this code are found the building blocks for a society based on social justice and equality:

> Do not strip your vineyards bare, nor gather the overlooked grapes; you must leave them for the poor and the stranger — I, **the Lord, am your God** ... You must not steal, you must not act deceitfully nor lie to one another... **I am the Lord.** You must not oppress your neighbor. Do not commit robbery. The wages of your laborer must not remain with you overnight until morning. Do not curse the deaf, nor put a stumbling block before the blind... **I am the Lord.** Do not pervert justice, neither by favoring the poor nor by deferring to the powerful... You must not go about slandering your kin, nor may you stand idly by when your neighbor's blood is being shed — **I am the Lord** (*Leviticus*, ch. 19, vs. 10-16).

It is true that to stand idly by while someone commits a sin, and to do nothing about it, most certainly implicates the bystander, thus debauching the idea of the "innocent bystander." One is reminded of the final episode of the Seinfeld comedy series, where Jerry and his three cohorts, George, Elaine and Kramer, stuck in a small fictitious New England town, witness a robbery, and not only do nothing to stop it, but laugh as it takes place. Under the town's "Samaritan Law," they stand accused of being "innocent bystanders," but as their engaging attorney, Jackie Chiles, points out: "How can an 'innocent' bystander be guilty"? However, if we take seriously the exhortation from the Levitical Holiness Code, "...

nor may you stand idly by when your neighbor's blood is being shed," then there is little question the Seinfeld-four are truly guilty.

What does it mean not to stand idly by when your neighbor's blood is being shed? Is this not a call for action? Moreover, if we know that our neighbor's blood is about to be spilled, should we not assume a preemptive stance and strike at the alleged attacker before he or she carries out an act of tragic proportions? Was not the U.S. war on Iraq predicated on just such a premise? In the *Talmud*, it is written: "When someone comes to kill us, we are obligated to kill him first" (*Sanhedrin* 72a). But this text is highly qualified by Maimonides, who held that killing an assailant in self-defense is justified only when the threat to one's life is imminent. If such justification cannot be proven, the presumed victim can be charged with a capital crime.

It would then seem that acts of revenge are Divinely forbidden despite God's behavior, which often seems both vindictive and arbitrary. But, since every one of God's admonitions from the Levitical Holiness Code rails against acts of vengeance — notice that each commandment is followed by the declaration "I am the Lord" (or some variation of the same Divine theme) — it is obvious that we have a classic case of: "Do as I say, not as I do." Yet, even here there are inconsistencies, as God orders the Israelites, in the process of fulfilling the Divine promise to "inherit the land," to carry out what can only be considered some pretty vengeful acts.

The best way to close this section, and to lead us to the next question, is to quote two biblical passages:

I recognize my transgressions and am ever conscious of my sins (*Psalms* 51:5).

He who conceals his transgressions shall not prosper, but he who confesses and forsakes them shall obtain mercy (*Proverbs* 28:13).

It should be crystal clear that we need to acknowledge our sins, but it is less obvious that we will "obtain mercy" because of our admission of wrongdoing. It almost seems that if God has His or Her way, our wrongdoings might just as easily instigate a process of collective punishment as initiate a process of shared forgiveness. At times, it almost seems that there is a whimsical response on God's part to our transgressions.

Who bestows upon us a measure of mercy? What is mercy? Is it a form of pity, of sympathy, of clemency? Who needs it? All we essentially need is to be forgiven by our friend for talking behind his or her back, so that we can stop feeling guilty. It matters little whether we believe in original sin or acquired sin or societal sin or preordained sin; we all err ("To err is human; to repent, divine; to persist, devilish" — Benjamin Franklin, 1706-1790). What is ultimately important is that we do something about it; and, even if the process of asking forgiveness is predetermined, does it ultimately matter?

If belief in God, however one defines that belief, or however one defines God, can prompt a process of genuine repentance for sins committed, then the role of a Deity in our lives can only serve for the good. The question we have to ask ourselves is: How can we determine what God wants from us, given the inconsistencies in the Almighty's words and behaviors? How does sin intersect with guilt and responsibility?

What is the Relationship Between Guilt and Responsibility?

To blame God for that which goes wrong in our lives is to essentially say that we are not at fault. A "true believer" would be offended by such a thought, for God is not only blameless, but most certainly, faultless. For those who reject the idea of a God altogether, the burden of responsibility for anything that happens must rest entirely with the initiator of an action. As for those who have yet to make up their minds whether to believe in a Higher Being or not, their vacillation may serve them the best. When they want to escape the responsibility for something unfortunate that happens, they can simply blame the God in Whom at that moment they believe. At the same time, when they want to accept credit when things go well, they can give themselves a pat on the back, as if God did not exist. This is "convenient theology."

Of course, this approach to belief becomes far more complicated when something occurs that is beyond our control. Take, for example, my sudden illness. I do not believe that there was anything seriously lacking in my life, or that I did something terribly wrong that prompted my disease. Let us suppose that I did accept such a view, did my punishment have to be so definitive? Wouldn't the removal of a kidney or a lung have been sufficient? I would have been severely limited, but not eliminated! Then again, in my case things happened so fast that it is only now, after the fact, that I can ponder such matters, excluding the possibility of correcting my faults. I have been stripped of any corrective powers I may have possessed. And yet, when I ponder reality, there was probably nothing I could have done to alter my fate. There are too many things in our lives that are simply beyond our control.

There is a fierce prayer that is recited on Judaism's most sacred holiday, *Yom Kippur,* the Jewish Day of Atonement, a day devoted to self-examination and inner contemplation:

> On *Rosh HaShana* [the New Year] it is written,
> On *Yom Kippur* [ten days after *Rosh HaShana*] it is sealed –
> How many shall pass on, how many shall come to be;
> Who shall live and who shall die;
> Who shall see ripe old age and who shall not;
> Who shall perish by fire and who by water;
> Who by sword and who by beast;
> Who by hunger and who by thirst;
> Who by earthquake and who by plague;
> Who by strangling and who by stoning;
> Who shall be secure and who shall be driven;
> Who shall be tranquil and who shall be troubled;
> Who shall be poor and who shall be rich;
> Who shall be humbled and who shall be exalted.

As much as we try to, and should, take control of our lives, there are many aspects which we do not have the ability to control, as this prayer so powerfully indicates. We can influence the quality of our life, and our disposition can contribute to our stability, but there are so many variables beyond our control that shape what happens to us. The person who smokes three packs of cigarettes a day or drinks extensively may hasten his or her demise (although not necessarily). But, our final day of reckoning is generally beyond our control. What makes this particular prayer so poignant is that it touches upon the unpredictable — what might happen from one year to the next. This year we may be secure, but next year we may be driven; this year we may be tranquil, but next year we may be troubled, this year we may be alive, but next year we may be dead.

So, why do I feel guilty that I am leaving my family "high and dry"? Worse, why do they feel so guilty? You know, the usual stuff: "I never showed my appreciation for all that he did; we should have scratched his back when he asked..." (I could ask these same questions of myself in relation to my family.) I wish I could tell them that they do not need to feel guilty. I had the perfect family — except for the back-scratching. I really did, and, because they were so loving, I feel terribly responsible for their future, even though I can't do a thing about it. Talk about guilt! At this moment, there is nothing that would give me more satisfaction than to blame God. But, what good would that do for me or my family? It would only make me feel worse than I already do. Could it be that no one is responsible for my early departure from this world?

The truth is that we all walk around with a guilt complex. If God is responsible for one human emotion that He or She planted in us mortals, no better one than "guilt" could have been devised. I do have a thought though: While guilt plays an integral role in the way individuals behave within the context of their family or their immediate community, it seems to play far less of a role when an individual obtains a position of power or undue influence. How a political leader can go to sleep at night, after sending children off to wage war, and not feel incredibly guilty is beyond me — unless that leader feels the absolute rightness of the cause. And, if someone possesses such assuredness, then that person is either a fool or lying to him- or herself. Then again, there are those leaders who invoke God's name for what they are doing. I am not referring to the time of the Crusades, I am speaking about today, when American presidents send their citizens off to war, even if such an act is geopolitically justified, with the words: "May God be with you," or

"So help me God," or "God bless." Invoking God's name may be the only way to assuage their guilt, but ultimately such Divine exploitation will not provide them with peaceful sleep, unless they are totally insensitive. A measure of guilt is bound to disturb their rest. The question is whether even a modicum of guilt would inform their decisions. It certainly should force one to own up to his or her responsibility for having others execute a fateful decision.

"Control guilt and you control the child," wrote humorist Dan Greenberg. He adds: "Let your children hear you sigh every day; if you don't know what they have done to make you suffer, they will"! Sigmund Freud (1856-1939) identified guilt as an inescapable stumbling block in a child's development as he or she goes through an Oedipal or Electra phase. The child falls in love with the parent of the opposite sex, thus desiring the elimination of the parent of the same sex, and thereby diffusing anxiety and guilt. Normally, this is worked out during latency. Sometimes it is not, leaving a residual guilt complex. This legacy of repressed, unconscious and neurotic feelings of guilt often leads to poor personality teamwork, hampering the effective functioning of the super-ego (what we call conscience) when confronting the libido (what we might call the pleasure principle). The result is a crippling self-reduction in the Marxian (Groucho) sense: "I wouldn't want to belong to any club that had me as a member."

Woody Allen once wrote: "My only regret in life is that I'm not someone else"! Referring to this lack of self-acceptance, the noted Glaswegian psychoanalyst, R.D. Laing, the author of *The Divided Self* and *The Politics of Experience*, commented:

> True guilt is guilt at the obligation one owes to oneself to be oneself. False guilt is guilt felt at not being what other people feel one ought to be or assume one is.

There are a variety of paths taken by people suffering from guilt complexes: Some punish themselves, never allowing themselves to succeed in anything; others do penance; and still others engage in a compulsive manner in various kinds of religious rituals, almost in a fetish fashion, continuously atoning for their sins — with the maxim that more is necessarily better.

All of the above can lead to one bearing too much guilt, which may be objectively unjustified, and often undefined, festering in the unconscious and possibly destroying one's psychic well-being. The Roman historian Livy noted: "Men's minds are very ingenious in palliating guilt in themselves" (Titus Livius, 59 B.C.E. — 17 C.E.). Such an attitude has seemed to climax in our own day, as we have been raised on the popular philosophy: "I'm OK, you're OK"; "Everyone's doing it, I'm no sucker"; "I need my space"; "That's the way I am, take me or leave me"; and "Don't lay a guilt trip on me." An atmosphere of permissiveness breeds indolence, indulgence, rationalization and repression. By absolving ourselves of guilt, we also relieve ourselves of responsibility. What remains is selfishness, material acquisitiveness and the inability to defer gratification. With the adoption of such an attitude, there is often a substantial lack of personal accountability, the super-ego having been bought off. Here, there is simply no guilt.

We have now set up a dialectic, which on the one hand deals with too much guilt, and on the other hand with not enough guilt. We must find a synthesis of just the right amount of healthy, justified, conscious and non-neurotic guilt. Such a synthesis between the thesis of too much guilt and the antithesis of not enough guilt requires an Aristotelean "Golden Mean," a middle path that leads to a sound and educated super-ego, which is essential to healthy development. Humankind's moral improvement depends on the recognition that there is a relationship between guilt and responsibility. The story is told of a psychiatrist, who, after examining a patient, informs him: "There is nothing the matter with you. You do not have an inferiority complex — you are inferior"! It is not that we are paranoiac, we all suffer from a guilt complex. We are guilty of misdemeanors, injustices, slights. There is such a phenomenon as objective guilt.

On *Yom Kippur,* as mentioned before, a Jew dedicates an entire day of prayer and introspection exclusively to guilt. The process of internalizing one's guilt and assuming responsibility, as practiced on this holiday, is very instructive and in some ways parallels the balance between sin and repentance. *Yom Kippur,* though rooted in the Old Testament, was a rather late holiday in its application, having been instituted less than two-and-a-half millennia ago, primarily as a ritual purgation of the Sanctuary of the High Priest. With the destruction of the Second Jewish Commonwealth by the Romans at the turn of the Common Era, Judaism began a process of maturation and democratization, wherein each Jew — both as an individual and as a member of the community — engaged in coming to terms with guilt and responsibility, sin and repentance. In everyday parlance, the partnership of guilt and responsibility is relegated to the human sphere, whereas the joining together of sin and repentance is considered an act that must be resolved in the Heavenly sphere.

Basically, the process employed to alleviate feelings of guilt entails redressing the wrongs done to another. Following this, and only following this, one is permitted to enter the synagogue and confess one's sins, with the help of a powerful finger-pointing liturgy. Then the individual can turn to God and plead for understanding and forgiveness, which is only granted once a New Year's resolution is made to shoulder responsibility for one's actions. This process of internalization is accompanied by a physical choreography, where a Jew is commanded to stand erect, and to beat his or her breast every time a particular transgression is acknowledged.

The demand to stand erect, not leaning on anything, symbolizes that one is not permitted to blame other people or circumstances for that which one should be personally accountable. (No room here for an "Officer Krupke" approach to guilt and responsibilty). By reciting a fixed formula, one is not shamed before his or her fellow worshippers. This is the reason that the "guilt offering" in biblical days, primarily for interpersonal sins, which externally looked like other sacrifices, was offered at the same place in the same way, in order not to shame one individual before others.

What about atoning for the sins of others? Since *Yom Kippur* is a day of self-examination, deprivation (there is a twenty-four hour fast, in which one is forbidden to eat or drink) and penitence, the dramatic themes and tones of this day force a Jew to engage in serious soul-searching. Jews are told that the quality of an individual's repentance will determine whether he or she will be inscribed in the "Book of Life" or the "Book of Death." While a Jew may not interpret this literally, the imagery should be sufficiently powerful to prompt a person into action, as one stands self-accused before the entire community. This explains why the litany of sins to which a Jew confesses on *Yom Kippur* is expressed in the plural:

> For the sins **we** have committed against You... have mercy on **us**, pardon **us**, forgive **us**... **we** have sinned, **we** have transgressed, **we** have gone astray.

In the prayer, simply entitled, "Confession," the entire community stands as one and its members literally beat their breasts, reciting an alphabet of sins beginning with:

> Arrogance, bigotry, and cynicism; and ending with: ... violence, weakness of will, xenophobia and misguided zeal.

It must be noted that all of the transgressions enumerated in the liturgy are those committed between people (ethical violations), and no mention is made of ritual transgressions against God. Perhaps God has greater patience for those who have failed to appreciate the necessity of ritual laws than for those who blatantly ignore the laws of morality. For those who disobey the laws of morality, guilt leads to shame, which explains why in many of the confessional prayers on *Yom Kippur,* one begins with the words: "We are ashamed."

While it would be nice to believe that we are motivated to alter our ways because we know that is the right thing to do, the harsh reality is that we are often shamed into doing what is right. Our motives are frequently less than altruistic. The plural form of the supplications, in which Jews articulate sins for which they may personally not have committed, must, according to Jewish understanding, follow this *Talmudic* dictum:

> Whosoever has the capacity to prevent his household from committing a crime and does not, he is accountable for the crimes (sins) of the entire household... (*Shabbat* 54b).

This is an excellent argument for both universal and collective guilt. I might add that concern for some sort of Divine scolding for our sins could serve as a positive influence.

While *Yom Kippur* has a lonely quality to it, one's repentance for sins takes place within a larger context, leading to the fast of *Yom Kippur,* which is explained in verses from *Isaiah* that are read on the Holy Day:

> Is this the fast I look for? A day of self-affliction? Bowing your head like a reed, and covering yourself with sackcolth and ashes? Is this what you call a fast, a day acceptable to the Lord? Is not this the fast I look for: To unlock the shackles of injustice, to undo the fetters of bondage, to let the oppressed go free, and to break every cruel chain? Is it not to share your bread with the hungry, and to bring the homeless poor into your house? When you see the naked, to clothe them, and never stand idly by, hiding yourself from your own kin (58:5-7)?

The message here is quite clear, while one might not be specifically guilty of the sins committed by the community at large, he or she bears some responsibility. The act of expiation is defined as a collective one, and therefore, seeking repentance is a collective endeavor. In the words of Abraham Joshua Heschel: "If we are not all guilty, we are all responsible."

One might inquire: Why do we have to confess that for which we feel guilty before God? And now, we are confronted once again with that age-old theological dilemma: Doesn't the omniscient One know what we have done wrong? The Almighty is not the Dan Greenberg prototype personality who sighs every time we enter a place of worship, so that if God doesn't know what we have done to feel guilty, we will. What is vital to our discussion is that we, as individuals, in a collective setting, bring to our conscious mind all our guilt feelings, so that we can recite with the Psalmist: "I recognize my mistakes and am ever conscious of my guilt" (51:5). More to the point: "He who hides his transgressions shall not prosper; but he who forsakes them, pleading guilty, shall obtain mercy" (*Proverbs* 28:13). Simply put, guilt is necessary for our own mental well-being.

The very fact that we should feel guilty not only for certain aspects of our own behaviors, but also for others' actions, necessarily places personal responsibility on the front burner. Only the assumption of responsibility can lead to corrective behavior. A measure of guilt, both imagined and real, prompts greater accountability and thus increased dependability. Better yet, individual guilt leads not only to individual responsibility, but more significantly, to collective loyalty.

But, what do we do with this statement that appears in the first of the Ten Commadments:

> … for I, the Lord your God, am an impassioned God, visiting the guilt of the fathers upon the children, upon the third and fourth generations of those who reject Me, but showing kindness to the

thousandth generation of those who love Me and keep My
commandments (*Exodus* 20:5-6).

The problem with this verse is quite obvious. The very notion that
my great-great grandchildren should suffer for my sins is terribly
unfair. Is this what is called "Divine Justice"? If so, it is a good thing
that we mortals altered such a prejudicial view in our legal system.
Only the actual guilty person is punished for a particular crime, not
that person's offspring. The children of a criminal may suffer guilt
by association, and, if that is what God meant, it would be
acceptable. Anything more than that would be objectionable.
Therefore, what is redeeming about this Divine warning is that it
should give us all pause to consider our actions and behavior, as
they may have a snowball effect, lingering on from one generation
to the next, implicating our children. Then again, the converse is
true, as it is also written that kind acts last for generations.

And yet, despite this dire forecast of future generations
suffering the consequences of present-day behavior, once again we
find a compelling example to the contrary — one more of those
Divine inconsistencies, and proof that God can actually change His
or Her mind. Such was the case in God's treatment of Ishmael,
Abraham's older son, by way of his handmaiden, Hagar. Abraham's
wife, Sarah, afraid that she was barren, encourages Abraham to
impregnate Hagar to guarantee the perpetuity of the Jewish people,
as promised by God to Abraham. In the Bible's cryptic report of the
story of Ishmael, we hear that the boy's behavior is so intolerable
that Sarah beseeches Abraham to drive Ishmael and his mother
from the house. Abraham appeals to God, recognizing the injustice
of Sarah's demand, but, God tells Abraham that he should do as
Sarah urges. So, reluctantly, he sends them into the wilderness —
with only bread and water.

Soon mother and son lose their way and, having no more food
and drink, face a bitter end. Tears streaming down her cheeks,

Hagar places the whimpering child in the shade of desert shrubs, looks away so as not to watch his suffering, and prays for help. Then, we read:

> God heard the cry of the boy, and an angel of God called to Hagar from heaven and said to her: "What troubles you, Hagar? Fear not, for God has heeded the cry of the boy — **where he is.** Come, lift up the boy and hold him by the hand, for I will make him a great nation." Then God opened her eyes and she saw a well of water. She went and filled the skin with water, and let the boy drink. God was with the boy and he grew up... (*Genesis* 21:17-20).

While it is a most admirable Divine lesson that we should judge people against their present behavior and action, all of us carry our history, often weighted down by an historical nemesis, not of our making; thus, the painful truth that future generations do suffer for our transgressions. When it comes to nations, there is natural syllogistic fallout. Consideration by a nation before it enacts certain policies, both domestic and foreign, is critical for those who will have to live with the consequences of that nation's actions.

Yet, despite the inherent logic that we all suffer from the consequences of previous behaviors, a theological modernist would say that God has permitted us to go astray, but has given us the free will to stand up and be counted, so we alone bear the full responsibility for our misdeeds. Does it matter whether guilt, shame or previous behaviors on our part or the part of others motivates us to assume responsibility? Probably not, but how rewarding it would be to assume responsibility, individually and collectively, without any prior emotional baggage to serve as a trigger. How do we get to such a point of purity of action, of unselfish commitment? We may have to explore the theory that there is a Spark of Divinity in each of us.

Question #21

Does God Know Our Thoughts?

Admittedly, the discussion in the previous two questions may be just a healthy intellectual exercise. Most of us are neither philosophers nor sociologists, although we can appreciate the importance of both disciplines in trying to understand human behavior. Indeed, behavioral psychology is quite helpful in breaking certain debilitating physical habits and modifying disabling psychological traits. However, the question on which I obsess, and to which I must obtain an answer, is: Could I have done anything differently in my life to prevent my early demise, or was it all predetermined and immutable? Here the conflict between Determinism and Free Will matters very deeply.

Simply put, if God knows all, then everything that happens to us, from womb to tomb, is fated. If someone knows our thoughts, then it is impossible for us to be "free thinkers." We may want to "think" otherwise, but we would be merely fooling ourselves. As indicated earlier, prayer is the means by which a believing person expresses his or her faith in a Higher Being. Again, it is Maimonides who wrote in his *Thirteen Articles of Faith*:

> I believe with complete faith that the Creator, Blessed be His Name, **knows the deeds of all human beings and their thoughts,**

as it is said, "He fashions their hearts all together; He comprehends all their deeds."

Such an all-encompassing theological outlook is pretty devastating. If one adopts such a ubiquitous point of view, well and good. But, for those of us who never accepted Divine control over our thoughts and deeds, it comes as a bit of a shock. Could it be that we were laboring under an illusion, thinking that we actually had some influence over our lives? I wish someone had told me early on that this was not the case. Then I could have prepared better for my early departure from this world. Had I known what was in store for me, that my life would come to a standstill so abruptly, I would have been able to plan more resourcefully. I feel that I may be leaving my family in the lurch. They will now have to scramble around to piece their lives together in a post-husband, father, grandfather world, not just emotionally, but financially. I never fully enlightened them as to our financial assets or the source of my pension, which is their rightful inheritance. Maybe it is just as well, for they will have to busy themselves with bureaucratic details, diverting their thoughts from full occupation with my death.

So, what are we to do to put our house in order? Well, first of all, there is that wonderful notion that is found in the *Mishnah*:[1] "Repent the day before you die" (*Ethics of the Fathers* 2:14). The question is: How can we know with certainty that we have reached the pen-ultimate day of our life? We don't, therefore we should repent everyday, for tomorrow the proverbial angel of death may come tapping on our shoulder. Basically, it does us little good to rehearse our life over and over again, wondering how we might

---

1. The codification of Jewish law, the *Mishnah* was compiled by Judah HaNasi around 200 C.E. It contains the basis for Oral Law, traditionally given to Moses at Mount Sinai and handed down by word of mouth, side by side with the *Torah*, from generation to generation. The *Mishnah* is divided into six parts (orders), each one being divided into tractates, and each tractate divided into sections, which in turn contain paragraphs; also called *Mishnayot*.

have done things differently, for it can only frustrate us, especially if everything is subject to a Divine *fait accompli*. It is simply not helpful to live a life of "what ifs."

Ultimately, I think that we would all like to subscribe to the Frank Sinatra philosophy of life as articulated in his signature song, *My Way*: "Regrets, I've had a few, but then again, too few to mention." Would that we could all have few regrets, believing that well-worn phrase: "If I had to do it all over again, I wouldn't change a thing." But, this would depend on us thumbing our noses at Divine control. Here is where Ole' Blue Eyes, the prime cheerleader of the advocates of Free Will, puts all to shame: "I planned each chartered course, each careful step along the byway. But more, much more than this, I did it my way." If this world-view is not a slap in the face to the theists, those Divine determinists, I don't know what is.

There has to be an answer that mediates between a God Who is omniscient and still allows for some maneuverability on our part — to do it our way, at least, partially. Let us imagine a game of chess. When, on May 21, 1997, chess grandmaster Gary Kasparov played against Big Blue, an IBM computer that simply processed everything at blinding speed, there should have been no doubt of his defeat. We are told that machines have finally learned to think and, "God forbid," out-think us. Because one of the greatest chess players of all time could not beat the computer, we are told, "Woe is our fate." But there is one Being Who can tame even the smartest computer: God. God is the "Mother" of all grand chessmasters, capable of defeating Bobby Fisher, Gary Kasparov and Big Blue blindfolded. It is God Who sets before us all the possible options that each player could choose, but allows us to ultimately make the choice — some better and some worse — which would explain evil in our world without necessarily implicating God.

God is like the erstwhile phone operator who could plug in a line and listen to any conversation. Or better yet, like the old *George*

Burns and Gracie Allen Show (1950-1958), in which George would go upstairs, turn on an in-house TV, and find out exactly what his wife Gracie was scheming. In modern terms, if He or She would want, God could enter into everyone's computer or bug everyone's phone — being a sort of Orwellian "Big Brother." But God chooses not to, in order to give to His or Her creatures flexibility to determine their fate — free from theistic direction, but not free from natural causality.

According to Israeli law, when children receive a driver's license, for the first two months they must drive with a parent. After that, they are free to drive on their own. However, they must place a sign in the rear window of the car that reads: "New Driver," which can be removed only after a full year of driving. The chances are that, during this initial trial period, they will make mistakes — minor accidents, insignificant bumps, slight scrapes. It will take time until they can navigate the roads by themselves. Perhaps that is what God wants for us: To learn from our mistakes, so that we will eventually "come into our own," thinking and acting without parental/Godly interference and supervision.

As music is math made beautiful, chess is math made obvious. What is complicated to us is commonplace to God. Therefore, it would seem that God places before us all the musical intricacies and possibilities to compose a wondrous symphony or a demonic cacophony.

Even if God is fooling us into thinking that we make our own decisions, what difference can it make if we are so duped that we are unaware of this Divine trickery? What would be the matter with living in a little ignorant bliss, believing that we, based on our independent knowledge of the game of chess, know best to move the knight to overtake the bishop?

How Do We Distinguish between Right and Wrong?

Believe in the power of Jesus, follow His example, and you can do no wrong; learn the teachings of the *Koran,* and you will follow in the path to righteousness; study *Torah* and it will lead you to good deeds; worship the Buddha and you will find the good in yourself. How many times have we heard the finest priests, kadis, rabbis and monks preach this ethic: "Faith in God (Jesus, Allah or Buddha) is all we need to live a life of goodness." Life's choices should only be that simple.

While certainty is preferable to ambiguity, is there anyone who is justifiably one hundred percent sure of his or her decisions and actions? Borrowing from the previous question, it is simply unfair that only God be omniscient, a prerequisite for self-assuredness, which, in turn, is a precondition for distinguishing between right and wrong (although we all know a number of "know-it-alls").

> See, I have set before you this day, life and goodness, death and evil... I have put before you life and death, blessing and curse. Choose life — that you and your offspring shall live... (*Deuteronomy* 30:15,19).

Being perpetually suspended between right and wrong, good and bad, life and death is difficult to cope with. Sure, there may be some obvious choices, but there are many more obscure ones. If God would only deal in gradations, in compromise, in nuance, both God and we would be better off. God may have a firmer grasp on moral behavior than we mortals, but given some of the choices the Almighty has made, as recorded in the holy literature of all the major religions, it seems God gets a bit confused between what is "right" and what is "power." It is as if God is always trying to prove that He or She is right by "kicking sand in our faces."

The notion that we should not follow the Divine example in distinguishing between right and wrong is pretty difficult to swallow. Nations seem to take their cue from God when waging wars of destruction. Just look at what the Almighty did not only to Sodom and Gomorrah, but also to all those nations that fought each other during the biblical reign of the Israelite kingdoms.

Let me cite a personal example of a position in which I found myself that clearly defines the challenges in discerning between right and wrong. In June of 1982, my army reserve unit was called into action, as Israel waged war against Lebanon, ostensibly to put a stop to Palestinian terrorists firing rockets into Israel's northern border towns. Before crossing over into Lebanon, our commanding officer told us:

> As soon as you enter Lebanon, you will pass a twelve-mile stretch of banana fields opposite the sea. There will be elderly Lebanese women picking the bananas, but, behind each one of them will be a PLO (Palestinian Liberation Organization) operative, using them as human shields as they fire their self-propelled grenades at your tanks. You are to wear your helmets, put on your flak jackets, cock your M-16 semi-automatic rifles, shoot first and ask questions later!

Crossing the border into southern Lebanon, we could see through our telescopes the Palestinians our commander was talking about, literally hiding behind Lebanese women tending their fields, as they fired those self-propelled grenades at our tanks. For the entire twelve-mile stretch, there was not a minute of respite from the constant firing. And yet, we never turned our cannons or our personal weapons on the Palestinians, for fear of killing someone who was innocent. It was only later when we took up our positions above the Beirut-Damscus highway that we learned that one of the tanks in our unit was hit, and that two of my comrades-in-arms, with whom I had served in the army since basic training, had been killed.

No one can comfort me by telling me I did the right thing. There was no right and wrong. When visiting the widows, we did not tell them the circumstances in which their husbands were killed. Amnesty International might have lauded us, but why was it that I did not feel I occupied the moral high ground? Perhaps the morally right thing would have been to shoot back. I know that I will never forgive myself for actually killing a Palestinian in Lebanon, but then it seemed to me a clear choice of "either him or me." But, upon reflection, realizing that Israel should have never entered Lebanon in the first place, guilt still plagues me. That might not be the case with someone else who felt that the war was justified.

Now comes the question: What motivates one to do that which is right? Are the reasons pure or selfish? I admit that my involvement in an organization called Israeli Rabbis for Human Rights was not necessarily motivated by an unselfish concern for the rights of the Palestinians who are living under Israeli occupation. Mostly I wanted to bring about a change that would enable my children to live a normal life without the fear of being blown up by a suicide bomber when going to the local supermarket. I think that most of my engagement in the human rights and peace movements was motivated by deep personal concerns: I did not want (and still do not want) my daughters, or more accurately, their spouses, to be confronted with the real life and death moral dilemmas that I confronted, and that still haunt me. Then again, who is to say that my approach is the correct one? Maybe bombing terrorists back to the Stone Age is the proper response. Could it be that dropping atomic bombs on Hiroshima and Nagasaki was justified because it abruptly ended the war with Japan, perhaps saving many thousands of lives?

Unfortunately, there is little Divine guidance here. Believing in the power of Jesus, learning the teachings of the *Koran*, studying *Torah* or worshipping the Buddha does not necessarily set us on the path of righteous behavior. One has to cull from the wealth of sacred literature those moral preachings that direct us to acts of decency and loving kindness. But, everything is subject to human interpretation; in the words of Paul Simon's song: *One Man's Ceiling is Another Man's Floor.*

For example, in the Middle East, the burden of history has often presented a formidable obstacle to peace. It seems virtually impossible to gain a common reading of the history of the Israeli-Palestinian conflict. Facts, events, and even statistics have been selected and manipulated to "build a case" or support predetermined positions. Two courses on the Middle East, taught respectively, by a pro-Israeli professor and a pro-Palestinian professor, are sure to diverge so sharply from each other as to make one wonder whether the same subject matter is being discussed.

Selective understandings of history, which appear to sustain contradictory judgments on the justice of one or the other cause, are often dismissed as propaganda, even if they do contain elements of truth. Maybe, therefore, it is impossible to render an impartial judgment when faced with competing choices. While it is convenient to rely on social norms to determine behavior, often a majority opinion can lead to a corruption of moral standards. A reason to outlaw the death penalty is the not uncommon travesties of justice, whereby a victim is sent to the electric chair for a crime that he or she did not commit. Because social norms can vary so dramatically from one society to another, and from one era to the next, we are told that the standards set by God are universal in nature, not subject to the confines of societal dictates or limited to specific historical time-frames. God is the First and the Last.

> I believe with complete faith that the Creator, Blessed is His Name, is the very first and the very last (Maimonides' *Thirteen Articles of Faith*).

If there are universal standards that have Divine backing, why should indecision play such a significant role in our lives when we are faced with moral choices? Of course, if we believe that God determines everything, that is a different story; or, is it? As previously mentioned, even if there is no way that we can ultimately know for certain whether we can control our own destiny or not, why not just plunge ahead anyway, trusting in our inherent goodwill to do that which is right? But what does it mean to know inherently the right thing to do?

Let us go back to the story of the Creation. Adam and Eve have two sons: Cain and Abel. Legend has it that Cain, jealous of Abel because his offering/sacrifice to God was more acceptable, kills his brother. He then immediately runs and hides. Why? There is no concept yet of death, and, most certainly, not of murdering or killing (a distinction between the two is made, for in the Ten Commandments, the Hebrew reads: "You shall not murder," implying that killing may be justified in some cases, such as in self-defense). Did Cain intuit that it was simply wrong to kill, that such an act of violence was contrary to the very laws of nature? Why should he have been so fearful of God's retribution? Fear often puts the brakes on wrongful behavior. Who told him that he did something wrong? Did his conscience suddenly get the better of him?

There is another troubling aspect to this story: Why would God create a human being capable of such an act of vengeance? Was it to serve as an explanation to generations of the violent retaliation for acts committed by one person against another, or one nation against the other? Does this support the notion of original sin, or is God simply letting human beings operate according to their own conscience? "Let your conscience be your guide." This is a lovely thought, but there is an obvious problem with such a pithy aphorism. A suicide bomber carries out a murderous act as a matter of conscience, warped as his or her conscience may be. In a court of law, jurists are asked to make judgments based upon the facts, not on their conscience. It is precisely for this reason that we have laws. One person's conscientious objection (ceiling) may be another person's conscientious agreement (floor). Of course, in Cain's case, he killed his brother, Abel, out of jealousy, one of the most destructive, though natural, of human traits. But, isn't God sometimes referred to as a "Jealous God"?

The entry of Free Will into the world is a grander Divine principle than Heavenly Determinism, even when issues of conscience or conviction vary from person to person, excluding both from playing any definitive role (perhaps a relative one) in distinguishing between right and wrong. But, murder? So soon after the creation of the human being? How can it be that the first naturally born human being kills the second naturally born human being?

Let us say that, in order to reduce the conflict between freedom of choice and theistic determinism, we should consider that choosing between right and wrong is not the power to do what one decides, but rather what one desires. The creation narrative would hold that the cause of our desires is to satisfy God, and we always act in accordance with these desires. Could it be possible then that Cain was merely implementing God's plan, much in the same way that perhaps Abraham did when he almost pulled a Lizzie Borden[1] on his son, Isaac? Was this the only way that God could bring to our

---

1. In a gruesome and sensational murder, in 1893, in Falls River, Massachusetts, "Lizzie Borden took an axe, and gave her mother forty whacks. When she saw what she had done, she gave her father forty-one."

attention a concept of death as against life? If so, God has quite a flair for the dramatic. And, if this were the case, should we then consider what Cain did as right, and not as wrong?

For the most part, we deal with issues of right and wrong on a much more trivial basis. Were we right to deprive our fourteen-year old daughter of her allowance because she got a belly-button ring without our permission? And, what about more subtle issues that are far less of a moral quandry: A wife is interested in painting the living room walls light blue while the husband is into beige. The next day, the wife comes home and discovers that the walls have assumed a disgusting hue of light brown — that abhorrent beige. Was the husband right in deciding unilaterally, against her will, because the sight of a light blue living room would have sent him into a fit of apoplexy? Maybe there is something of moral worth here, after all? A decision of this sort, that disregards the view of another, cannot be a right one. Apparently, in any decision we make, a delicate process of negotiations must take place, which can aid us in distinguishing between right and wrong. Every decision — political, social, religious, economic and even the most personal and seemingly humdrum — has its moral implications.

If we actually thought that every decision we make defined our moral character, then we would shy away from deciding anything. But most likely, if we genuinely considered the ethical components of our decision-making, we would be very careful in choosing a particular course of action over an alternative one. Moreover, it would be most desirable for nations to consider the moral implications of their decisions before committing themselves to a course of action, such as waging war, that might have irreversible moral consequences. Leaders who speak with moral certainty frighten me. It is only God who acts with moral self-assurance, and we should not presume to adopt such a Divine trait. But, given the fact that great leaders such as Abraham and Moses questioned God's lightning decisions, perhaps far less impressive figures such as ourselves might also dare to inquire of God as to why He or She did not take a little more time before wiping out virtually all of Noah's generation, setting only a remnant afloat in an ark for forty days and nights. Apparently, afterwards, God had second thoughts:

> I will maintain My covenant with you; never again shall all flesh be cut off by the waters of a flood, and never again shall there be a flood to destroy the earth (*Genesis* 9:11).

Can we ever know whether we chose the right or the wrong path, not only on issues of moral import, but also on matters of commonplace interest? In certain areas of life, the answer may be "yes." I know I made the right choice in my marriage because after more than thirty years together, I am still madly in love with my wife. This is not to say that disagreements did not occur along the way, like my deciding to paint that living room beige.

However, all of us live with uncertainty. But, who is to say that every choice we make must be definitive? Not all problems have solutions. Moral dilemmas and everyday decisions do not always lend themselves to easy answers of right and wrong. How one lives and copes with irresolution is critical. Indeed, it is this uncertainty, ambiguity and conflict that differentiate us from God. We are destined never to be fully confident in our opinions and actions. We often reach a moral impasse when it comes to choices between what we think is right or wrong. Sometimes we may feel that the choice is clear. Other times, we may be more hesitant, but a decision must be made. It is the latter that can cause us anguish. Whereas God may have no hesitations, it is good that we are prone to vacillation, providing that this does not lead to indecision or never-ending procrastination. Sometimes indecision can have far-reaching consequences. Silence can serve as a complicit partner for acts and behaviors — both positive and negative. Weighing the different options before choosing this or that path will make our decisions that much more informed and will decrease our level of anxiety over our choice.

Of course, the above discussion is all predicated on the proposition that not only can we at least try to distinguish between right and wrong, but we can also activate our free choice to either intuit or reason rightfully or wrongfully. Only such a thesis can excuse God from involvement in some of the more tragic events that have colored our lives — both personally and collectively.

What Does It Mean to "Blame God" or "Thank God"?

Why is it that when something goes wrong, we have a tendency to blame God, or conversely, when something goes right, the first words out of our mouths often are "Thank God"? When we stub our toe, why do we cry out: "Goddamnit" or "Jesus Christ"? Do we expect God to condemn the dining room table for getting in the way of our foot, or Jesus to ease the sting of the pain at the very moment we bang it on the corner of the bathroom door? What is this need to assess credit or blame for everything that happens? Is this merely a natural reaction or a subconscious yearning to remove from our shoulders the yoke of responsibility for certain events in our lives?

When my friend's daughter was born with cerebral palsy, he cursed the heavens. This was his first child. What went wrong? Of course, it was explained medically, but that did not satisfy him. His question was: Why my family? Of course, he was merely raising the point brought forth in earlier questions: Where was God — as if God were the determining force that caused his daughter's birth defect, which would leave her disabled for her entire life? The question of "where is God" is crucial to any discussion that deals with culpability and gratitude.

The most dramatic account of this question is found in Elie

Wiesel's book, *Night,* an autobiographical narrative of his experiences as a young boy in the Nazi concentration camps of Auschwitz and Buchenwald. He recounts one specific hanging that took place in the public square in Buna, a sub-camp of Auschwitz, also known as Buna-Monowitz or Auschwitz III. Wiesel writes: "I witnessed other hangings. I never saw a single victim weep... except once." He goes on to tell of an incident when an electric power station was blown up. The Gestapo, suspecting sabotage, found a trail leading to an *Oberkapo,* an SS appointed Jewish overseer of other Jews. Many of these *Oberkapos* were cruel, but this one, a Dutch Jew, who had seven hundred prisoners working under him, was loved like a brother because: "No one had ever received a blow at his hands, nor an insult from his lips."

The *Oberkapo* was arrested and tortured but refused to provide a single name of anyone who might have been involved in blowing up the power grid. He was transferred to Auschwitz and was never heard from again. The *Oberkapo* had a young boy working under him, a *pipel,* which was the designation for such young boys — "a child with a refined and beautiful face" — who was left behind. He too was tortured but remained silent. Finally, he was sentenced to death by the SS, along with two other prisoners. Wiesel finishes the story:

> One day when we came back from work, we saw three gallows rearing up in the assembly place, three black crows. Roll call. SS all around us, machine guns trained: The traditional ceremony. Three victims in chains — and one of them, the little servant, the sad-eyed angel...
>
> Three victims mounted together onto the chairs. The three necks were placed at the same moment within the nooses.
>
> "Long live liberty!" cried the two adults. But the child was silent.
>
> "Where is God? Where is He"?, someone behind me asked.
>
> At a sign from the head of the camp, the three chairs were

tipped over. Total silence throughout the camp. On the horizon, the sun was setting.

"Bare you heads!" yelled the head of the camp. His voice was raucous. We were weeping. "Cover your heads!"

Then the march began. The two adults were no longer alive. Their tongues hung swollen, blue-tinged. But the third rope was still moving; being so light, the child was alive...

For more than half an hour he stayed there, struggling between life and death, dying in a slow agony under our eyes. And we had to look at him full in the face. He was still alive when I passed In front of him. His tongue was still red, his eyes were not yet glazed.

Behind me, I heard the same man asking: "Where is God now"? And I heard a voice within me answer him: "Where is God? Here He is — He is hanging here on the gallows..."

This chilling account should have us wondering: Do we blame God for this horror? Do we hold God responsible for the death of one-and-a-half million Jewish children in the Holocaust? The Holocaust has altered the theological world-views of many Jews, as well as their ideological world-views, whereby Zionism[1] became the universal cause of most Jews throughout the world. It was Richard Rubenstein, in his seminal work, *After Auschwitz*, who articulated the problematics of the Jewish relationship to God after the death of six million Jews at the hands of the Nazis. We dare not thank God that it was not we who suffered such an unspeakable death as those during the Holocaust, although this is the most natural response

---

1. The national movement for the return of the Jewish people to their homeland and the resumption of Jewish sovereignty in the Land of Israel, Zionism advocated, from its inception, tangible as well as spiritual aims. Jews of all persuasions, left and right, religious and secular, joined to form the Zionist movement and worked together toward these goals. Disagreements led to rifts, but ultimately, the common goal of a Jewish state in its ancient homeland was attained, as decreed by the United Nations on November 29, 1947. The term "Zionism" was coined by Viennese Nathan Birnbaum (1864-1937), founder of *Kadimah*, the first organization of Jewish nationalist students in the West.

when we are spared from tragedy: "Thank God I am alive; I was supposed to be on that train when it crashed"! Such thoughts could drive us mad with guilt.

Asking the question "where is God" is merely a more sophisticated way of directing blame against God, instead of holding either ourselves or someone else responsible for an event of tragic proportions. It may make us feel good, accusing God for the evil in the world, but such an act of transference only serves as an analgesic, a temporary dulling of the senses. In the long run, it will not shield us from the anguish we feel or the pain we incur because of our own shortcomings or those of others. On the other hand, asking "where is God" is an expression of our inability to understand evil and misfortune. It can lead to a "crisis of faith."

It is interesting to note that a fervent believer would not use the word "blame" when addressing God. God is beyond blame, or rather, not subject to blame, for what the Almighty does or does not do belongs to the realm of the Divine. Either we are responsible for adverse events or God plots them in concert with some unknown or unrevealed Divine scheme. (Indeed, if we were to define religion, it would be the affirmation of God's design for the universe.) In either case, it would be simply wrong to point a finger at God. The only proper course that the ardent person of faith can take is the one that leads to "thanks" or "praise" for God's wondrous deeds. In short, we are to thank God when things go right, but never to blame the Lord when things go wrong.

Is There Such a Concept as a "Divine Spark"; and, if so, are We All Created Equal?

The statement, "we are all created in God's image," is vastly over-worked. To be perfectly frank, I am not sure what it means; and, given how I am feeling, particularly at this moment, I can't say that being created in a Divine image has any advantage. However, I do hope that the theological notion that God exists before and after time, that God is the First and the Last, will rub off on me.

To accept the idea that we are created in the Divine image means that imitating God is an enviable endeavor. Since, in previous questions, I have outlined some of the more untenable actions that God has taken, as well as some of the more contradictory positions that He or She has assumed, one might conclude that the Almighty is not necessarily the best role model. Possessing a "Divine Spark," as a result of being created in God's image, could either kindle a bright light or set off a consuming fire.

From the creation story, a person of faith understands that a Divine Spark is present within each and every one of us. Despite the waywardness of the generation of Adam and Eve, a Divine Spark was present in them. They just did not know how to cultivate it.

Upon waking in the morning, a Jew recites a prayer: "Thank

you, God, for returning the breath of life to me." When asleep, metaphorically, we are in the dark world of pre-creation:

> In the beginning God created the heaven and the earth. Now, the earth was unformed and void, and **darkness** was upon the face of the deep... (*Genesis* 1:1-2).

When we awake to the light of day each morning — light being the first thing that God created — it is as if the world had been created anew, as if God had breathed the same breath of air into us that He or She blew into Adam. This concept is reinforced in the morning prayer, where a Jew acknowledges God as the Creator:

> Blessed are You, O' Lord, our God, Ruler of the universe, Who... illuminates the earth and those who dwell upon it... and in Goodness, **renews, everyday, always**, the work of Creation.

For certain, if we took such a concept seriously, that the world is created anew, always, every day with our awakening, we would recognize that not only are we granted a fresh start every day, but that it is also incumbent upon us to do something dramatic with our lives. The exhortation here is for us to do something creative and worthwhile with our day, to make certain that what we do is elevating. What is called for is a forward pass, not a lateral one.

To further tie us into the creation story and the fashioning of human beings, we should note that God began the world with one person, Adam. Why was but a single person created? To emphasize an important social message that no one could boast his or her lineage or parentage to be greater than another person's. This is of great significance, for the idea of every person being a descendant of the same ancestor binds us together as brothers and sisters. While sibling rivalry dots the biblical narrative — Cain and Abel, Isaac and Ishmael, Jacob and Esau, Joseph and his brothers — perhaps the individual stories of these clashes are included as a matter of instruction to inform us of the consequences should we fail to recognize that we are all the offspring of one and the same person. And, most significantly, if it is God who created our universal parent, then God is the ultimate Parent. To behave in any manner that would be disrespectful of our brothers or sisters would mean to diminish part of the Divine Creation — the God within us.

According to the Jewish tradition, God created Adam from the dust of the earth so no one could say that he or she is made of superior stuff. In order that this would be understood in terms of race, we read in *Yalkut Shemoni*:[1]

> God formed Adam from the dust from all over the world — yellow clay and white sand, black loam and red soil — so that the no one can declare that a particular race or color of man does not belong here on earth, that this earth is not yours (on *Genesis* 2:6).

This gives some measure of equality to the expressions "from dust to dust," or "from ashes to ashes" or "from dust we come and to dust we return."

It can be inferred that, with God beginning the generations of men and women with a single person — in a most intimate way as recorded in the creation story — every one of us is a direct descendant of Adam. As such, we should have within us some of the Divine Spark that was breathed into him as the first human. The Spark may have substantially diminished with time, but the implication is that it is deeply ensconced within the recesses of our very being. We have to ask ourselves, given what we know about God, do we really want to cultivate that Spark or not?

What further support can we find for the notion of a Divine Spark within each of us? Catholicism embraces the theory of Transubstantiation, the process by which the bread and wine offered up at the holy communion of the Eucharist has its substance supposedly (perhaps miraculously) changed to that of the body,

---

1. A collection of commentaries on biblical passages, *Yalkut Shemoni* was compiled in Frankfurt — circa 1290 — by Rabbi Shimon Ashkenazi HaDarshan.

blood and soul of Christ. It is a visceral expression of both imbibing and eating the Divinity that is part of Jesus. Transubstantiation is also known as "the doctrine of the real presence," a not very euphemistic way of saying that a Divine Spark does in fact occupy a place within every Catholic, despite the concept of original sin.

The *Kabbalah*[1] expounds on the theory of the mystics, that before releasing a soul for life on earth, the Creator splits it in two. The male part enters the male child and the female part enters the female child. The idea of Divinity or spirituality or soul residing within us is religiously rooted. The skeptic will of course say that this is pure *poltergeist*. Souls being implanted in human beings, bread and wine being turned into the body and blood of Jesus? Whom are we kidding? But, are these religious beliefs so different from science's dallying with the Big Bang theory of the creation of the universe, where sparks or electrified atoms bounce off one another at random — one such accidental collision creating the world as we have come to know it? (Of course, there is the fear that there could be some molecular sparks still floating around that could collide and set off a blaze of destruction, which could end the world that we have come to know.) It's the chimpanzee theory of intelligence: Let a monkey sit in front of a word processor long enough, and eventually he will write a work of Shakespearean quality.

Whether one opts for the accidental theory of sparks as posited by physics, or an intentional implantment of sparks as held by the earnest believer, there probably is within each of us some measure

---

1. Hebrew for "tradition" or literally "receiving." *Kabbalah* is the overall designation for Jewish mysticism. The Kabbalists were first organized in sectarian circles. Before the thirteenth century, the term *Kabbalah* only referred to the writings of the prophets and Oral Law. The *Kabbalah* flourished in the fifteenth and sixteenth centuries, and was centered in the mountains of Safed in Israel. The Kabbalists believed that mystical doctrines were given to Moses at Mount Sinai and are hidden in the *Torah* and Oral Law. For Kabbalists, Divinity is pure and infinite, a spiritual light whose emanations account for all creation.

of immortality, which is obviously not realized physically. I would surmise that how one cultivates this Divine or Big Bang Spark, which reaches back to the incipience of humankind, is quite important. For the Big Bangers, that Spark we need to nurture cannot be defined in polar terms — good or bad. For the Divine Sparkers, a choice must be made between the contradictory traits that seem to characterize God's behavior and actions. This may be relatively easy to do if we choose certain personalities to emulate — personalities of those who supposedly spoke in God's name, personalities whose Divine essence should be accessible to us.

Here the choice could be pretty clear: Jesus over Judas, David the composer of *Psalms* over David the warrior. We need to seek out the more delicate side of our persona, making the bold assumption that, with all that Divine bravado, God is basically a pussycat, a sensitive soul, worthy of emulation. If humans possess basic decency and goodness, and someone wishes to attribute that very goodness and decency to a Higher Being or to a free fall of millions of molecules; and if that attribution causes us to highlight elements of integrity, civility, graciousness and sensitivity, which reside within us, who cares whether they came about by accident or design?

I think that I basically buy into the theory of there being good in everyone. After all, if Anne Frank, the thirteen-year old victim of the Holocaust, can write in her diary, "I still believe that people are good at heart," who am I to dispute the concept of a Divine Spark? It only means that the burden falls upon us to uncover the Divine Spark within us that comprises positive energy, so that we can bring some sanity into an often insane world; even as others pervert that Divine Spark, bringing about evil in the world that causes the murder of an Anne Frank.

Here we are faced wth a real challenge, as we must call upon our human, not God-like, resources to distinguish between a good Divine Spark and a bad Divine Spark, for who says that a Divine

Spark is necessarily something of intrinsic worth? In Judaism this is referred to as either the *yetzer hatov* (good inclination) or the *yetzer hara* (evil inclination). Each battles with the other for predominance. We are left to determine which element of Divinity we wish to claim. In short, we decide which Divine attributes we want to emphasize — goodness, compassion, mercy, tolerance, forgiveness, righteousness and justice; or vengeance, mercilessness, malice, vindictiveness, tempestuousness and retribution. To be created in the Divine image essentially entails our dealing with competing forces within ourselves, as we humans are possessed of a complex personality. Right and wrong, good and bad, sanity and insanity often abide each other in one happy (or sad) discordant harmony.

We are filled with inconsistencies, ambiguities and contradictions. Body and soul, mind and matter, intellect and emotion can often work at cross purposes. Viennese psychiatrist, Viktor Frankl (1905–1997), in his book, *The Unconscious God*, developed a theory, which recognizes the possibility of God having access to us through our conscience. He wrote: "Conscience would be ineffective if it is only me speaking to myself. Conscience is experienced as a dialogue" (much like the case with Jacob struggling with an angel of God). Anyone who has experienced "pangs of conscience" knows the tension of conflict, with the ego contesting and resisting the pull of a commanding sense of "what I ought to do" with what, in fact, "I actually do." There is an "I" within each of us that wants the opposite of another "I" within us; the two cannot be identical. One "I" pulls in one direction and another "I" pulls in another direction.

It is up to us to choose the appropriate "I," and, according to Frankl, it is the appropriate "I" that has within it the Divine Spark. It is our conscience — scruples, principles, ethics, a sense of right and wrong — that gnaws at us to do that which is good and decent, and makes us feel guilty when we do not. For Frankl, and for most believers, that conscience is God. Ergo — Conscience equals Divine Spark.

This makes sense to me. I feel about my conscience the same way as I feel about the beginning of the world: It is incomprehensible, beyond the human mind to fathom; and so, just as I attribute the creation of the world to an undefined Higher Being, so too could I characterize my conscience as a derivative Heavenly trait – my very own Divine Spark.

Wait a minute. Something doesn't sound right. Maybe I am jumping to conclusions. Could I be barking up the wrong tree, equating my conscience with the Divine Spark, inherited at birth? Perhaps conscience has nothing to do with Divinity, but is merely a function of behavioral norms and social conventions. After all, much of our behavior is determined by the society in which we live and shaped by the culture with which we are identified. When we act in a way that upsets our social and cultural world, does not our conscience prick us, making us feel guilty? As I review my life, I can clearly see where I did things that most certainly challenged my conscience, not necessarily because they stood in contradiction to what God may have wanted for me, but rather because they were inconsistent with what I should have wanted for me.

I am soothed by the thought of a Divine Spark operating behind the scenes. But, who says that every time we do something meritorious, we have to transfer that merit to God? Again, why does God have to get the credit when we do things right, but we take the heat when we do things wrong?

If truth be told, it is very comforting to believe that, as decendants of Adam (and, it seems to me that the biblical account of Creation is as good as any other, including evolution), we have within us a Divine Spark. While, at this juncture in my life, I was hoping that I would come "face to face" with God, (following in the footsteps of one of my role models, Moses — *Deuteronomy* 34:10), having not found Him or Her anywhere in sight, I like thinking that a bit of Divinity resides within me.

Is Atheism a Viable World-View?

Almost all of the preceding questions assume that there is a God, and that God is the One and Only, and the same God for all peoples; therefore we all have within us a trace of Divinity, and a measure of Holy attibutes. But, what about the avowed non-believer? All my questions, as curious and doubting as they may be, basically affirm a belief in God, although ill-defined and confused. However, I have still yet to come up with satisfactory answers to my questions, especially as they apply to myself. And so, the time might be ripe to examine whether there is any validity to an atheistic view of the world.

To ascribe to atheism is not to believe in God. This is not to say that atheists are not believers, rather that their belief does not include any religious or philosophical concerns for a deity. The atheist simply has no use for theology and religion.

How can we ever be certain of God's existence, either empirically or emotionally? For the atheist, the answer is we can't. Indeed, the atheist would probably say that the proof of the non-existence of a "Superior Being" is that humankind is always seeking ways to prove God's existence.

The atheist gains support for his or her non-theological view from the fact that there is no physical proof of God's existence, that the very essence of a God concept is dependent on one's individual faith. Even if one were to point to the alleged resurrection of Jesus as physical proof of God's existence, the atheist would scoff at such a thesis, because the denial of a Higher Being is accompanied by the rejection of miracles. And, the atheist has one very strong argument: If God is all that He or She is cracked up to be, why is there so much misery and pain and tragedy in the world? If anything, the atheist would say that there are more compelling reasons not to believe in God than to believe in "It." The rebuttal that we are incapable of understanding God's "mysterious ways" and designs for us would be viewed by the atheist as a complete cop-out.

The argument that there are no atheists in foxholes is just a glib and smug way of explaining why that devout non-believer in my army unit literally started "praying his guts out" when Syrian rockets began landing on us during the Lebanon War. His was simply a natural reaction, devoid of belief, but full of fear — no more significant than when I, a practicing Jew, yelled out "Jesus Christ" when I stubbed my toe. Fear and pain can propel one at any particular moment in time to do things that defy logic. While I do not wish to get into this subject matter now, there is little question that fear is a major factor in belief in God (there are countless prayers telling us to "fear the Lord"). This very powerful human emotion is often abused by some preachers, who, like the fictitious Elmer Gantry,[1] literally try to "put the fear of God" in us.

An atheistic world-view generally comes about either through deliberate choice or from an inherent inability to believe religious teachings, which seem to the atheist literally incredible. It is not a lack of belief born out of simple ignorance of religious doctrine. A

---

1. Written by American Nobel laureate for literature, Sinclair Lewis (1885-1951), *Elmer Gantry* was a searing and satiric indictment of fundamentalist religion that caused an uproar upon its publication in 1927. The philandering bigger-than-life personality of Gantry came alive in Burt Lancaster's powerful portrayal of him in the film version of the book in 1960.

mere lack of belief in God does not adequately define the atheistic position. Atheists *actively* believe that God does not or cannot exist.

One should not confuse atheism with simple skepticism; that is, a basic disbelief in the existence of God. We could ask: Isn't disbelieving in God the same thing as believing God does not exist? Disbelief as a particular proposition does not necessarily mean that one does not believe it to be true. Not believing that something is true is not equivalent to believing that it is false; one may simply have no idea whether it is true or not.

The Greek philosopher, Epicurus (341-270 B.C.E.), might be considered the father of atheism. His concern with evil leads him to deny the possibility of a God in our world:

> Is God willing to prevent evil, but not able? Then he is not omnipotent. Is he able, but not willing? Then he is malevolent. Is he both able and willing? Then whence cometh evil? Is he neither able nor willing? Then why call him God?

Epicurus has something here. There is so much evil in today's world that it is difficult to believe in a God of goodness. What is so remarkable is that belief in God has lasted, and has overwhelmed atheism, considering the evil that not only exists in the Bible, but evil that allegedly emanates from God and is initiated by God. It is amazing that most people do not become atheists after reading the Bible. Anglo-American political theorist, Thomas Paine (1737-1809), wrote in his book, *The Age of Reason*:

> After the sermon was ended… I was revolted at what I heard… I moreover believe that any system of religion that has anything in it that shocks the mind of a child cannot be a true system.

While belief in God does not necessarily equal belief in the Bible, nevertheless to read some passages in both the Old and New Testaments lends credibility to Paine's claim.

What about this Divine exhortation:

> If a man has a stubborn and rebellious son... Then shall his father and mother... bring him out to the elders of the city... And all the men of the city shall stone him with stones, that he dies (*Deuteronomy* 21:18-21).

For those who object to a teacher rapping a student on the knuckles with a ruler:

> Withhold not discipline from a child; for should you beat him with a rod [scepter]; he shall not die. Beat him with a rod and you will save him from the grave (*Proverbs* 23:13-14).

Having difficulties with women:

> Women should remain silent in churches. They are not allowed to speak, but must be in submission, as the Law says. If they want to inquire about something, they should ask their own husbands at home; for it is disgraceful for a woman to speak in church (I *Corinthians* 14:34-35).

> "Have you allowed all the women to live"? He (Moses) asked them... "Now ... kill every woman who has slept with a man, but save for yourselves every girl who has not slept with a man" (*Numbers*, 31:17-18).

As for indentured servants (slaves):

> ... you shall take an awl [a small pointed tool for making holes, especially in wood and leather], and thrust it through his ear... and he shall be your servant forever (*Deuteronomy* 15:17).

And, for good measure, let us look at this New Testament quote on peace:

> Think not that I have come to send peace on earth: I came not to send peace, but a sword. For I have come to set a man at

variance against his father, and the daughter against the
mother... (*Matthew* 10:34-35).

Here we have the proof texts for discrimination against women and
children, as well as a rationale for slavery and war. Religions
certainly seem to adopt a prejudicial view that embraces sexism and
ageism. While universal women's suffrage finally came to the
United States in the 1900s, primarily realized in the female right to
vote, religious inequality still plagues too many religions. Clerical
privileges are not accorded to women in three major (branches of)
religions: Orthodox Judaism (Reform Judaism ordained its first
woman rabbi in 1972), Catholicism and Islam. And, have you ever
seen a woman in the Dalai Lama's entourage? Show me a statue of
Buddha that looks like a female. Not only are clerical roles denied to
women, but look at the dress code for women in the fundamentalist
Moslem and Orthodox Jewish communities — the less of a woman
you see, the better off you are; after all, they are all potential Eves,
just waiting to lure the innocent man into a web of sin. In a
traditional Jewish prayer book, a Jewish male prays every morning:
"Praised are You, O' Lord, for not making me a woman." This is not
a prayer intended to validate one's masculinity, it is purely a prayer
of superiority, as a Jewish woman does not direct praise to God with
equal words. She says: "Praised are You, O' Lord, for making me
according to Your Will."

I excluded from the above quotes that with which I have already
wrestled: God sending Abraham to institute child sacrifice, the
destruction of Sodom and Gomorrah and the ground swallowing
Korach because he dared challenge Moses' leadership. These three
incidents from the Bible alone should be sufficient to drive anyone
into the hands of atheism, if only for his or her own self-protection
and self-preservation. If evil in the world is the primordial system of
logic for building a case for atheism, then the evil that stems from
Divine instigation, as outlined throughout the biblical narratives,

most certainly provides the data for building that case. If God is a "man of war" (*Exodus* 15:3), then the atheist would say: How can one be so naïve as to believe in such mischievous nonsense? Better to deny the existence of a deity than to contend with the evil that can stem from a Higher Being. Don't tell atheists that they have yet to "see the light" or that they are infidels. They would respond that believers "live in darkness," relegating reason to a secondary role.

It is ironic that religion seems to supply atheists with their best arguments. Those who would try to counter an atheistic view by quoting contrasting sacred texts that relate to God would be viewed suspiciously. If God, a perfect Being, contradicts Him- or Herself, then, for the atheist, that is further proof of the utter foolishness of believing in a deity.

Because of their insistence on maintaining the constitutional separation of church (religion) and state, declared atheists often suffer for their non-belief. It is the atheists, primarily, but not solely, who have been at the forefront of the struggle to safeguard this separation in the American public school system, guaranteeing that not even "through a back door" will mandatory prayers be recited in the classroom. The best known atheist of our time (and the most maligned), Madalyn Murray O'Hair, has led the ongoing battle in the courts whenever there was a question that a school was crossing the delicate line that keeps religion separate from the educational system.

The debate I have with atheism is that it contradicts human nature — that is, the need for an individual to believe in something beyond him- or herself. The revered Orthodox rabbi and scholar, Joseph Soleveitchik (1903-1993), wrote a book entitled *The Lonely Man of Faith*. There are times in life, when a person feels terribly alone. My moment is right now, lying in my hospital room, unable to express my thoughts to those around me — my wife, my children, grandchildren, the doctor. I am unable to share my emotional pain. I need that Divine connection.

The atheist would say that such ruminations, during a state of anxiety, when one is fearful of the unknown, are illusory, a psychological mind-game to seek comfort, driven by desperation, not reason. However, in spite of all my questions, God seems very real. I find myself praying to God, even though I am aware of many of His or Her failings and contradictions. I am still hoping against hope that God may yet come through, finally "getting it right"; even though I know in my heart of hearts that in a few days I will die. Again, the atheist would respond that I am deceiving myself, and the fact that I will finally succumb to my inevitable fate is proof that God did not answer my prayers because there is no God. Further, the atheist would add that my need for faith at this crucial moment in my life created God. In other words, it is we human beings who create God *ex nihilo*, not that God created the world *ex nihilo*. One thing about atheists — for supreme doubters, they are very certain of themselves.

It is here that the atheist serves the believer, because he or she forces us to ask: Does the basic human need for faith make God a reality for everyone, or only make God real for the individual? Can belief alone make God exist?

So, what does an atheist believe in? If the atheist puts his or her trust only in other human beings, it would seem to me that this is obvious folly, for we can most certainly measure human frailties and limitations. Ultimately, the atheist still cannot come up with an alternative understanding of the beginning of time. It is relatively easy to deny the existence of a supernatural being; it is far more difficult to build a belief system that can explain that which is inexplicable. What do atheists affirm? Are they at all engaged in a search for a meaning to life, for a purpose to existence? Does chaos rule the universe, and, as such, are we abandoned, destined to living out our lives in a meaningless cosmos? A traditional definition of God, which includes as its basis a belief in a Higher Being capable of doing that which is impossible in our eyes, seems to serve the needs

of human beings much better than an atheistic ideology that funda-
mentally throws up its arms, and declares in Dickensian terms:
"Christmas – Bah, humbug." But one must remember, in the end,
even Eliezer Scrooge recognized the need for belief.

Atheists believe that humankind is responsible for what
happens on earth, thus placing their faith in people. While human
beings are capable of great good, they are also capable of incredible
evil. Given our seeming inability to learn from our mistakes, it
would seem more reasonable and logical to believe in a God who
just might be capable of doing something miraculous that would
save the human species from a rather deplorable track record.

I can tell you one thing for certain: Once someone denies the
existence of God, when facing death, he or she becomes "the lonely
man of 'no' faith." As for me, I am still conducting my dialogue,
trying to figure out what went wrong — not with my fellow human
beings, but with God. As expressed in a Jewish prayer: "God
maintains faith with those who sleep in the dust." I am trying to see
how this Divine maintenance of faith works. Trust me, it is better to
believe in something, even if it be a "figment of the imagination."

One last comment: Jogging is supposed to be an excellent
exercise to preserve one's health. But, have you ever seen a jogger
smile while jogging? Such is my experience with atheists. They are
often negative, real "downers," humorless. They seem to be
eternally glum — dour personalities, devoid of hope. I can
understand why, because in the words of comedian Henny
Youngman (1906-1998): "Atheists have no holidays." If there is
nothing to celebrate or commemorate, or believe in, life can be
pretty dull.

Is God Dead?

Scratched into the bathroom stall at Cronin's Bar in Harvard Square (circa 1962) were the words: "God is dead, Nietzsche." The clever ivy-leaguer who scribbled that graffiti might have been a bit too confident. One could probably assert with a greater degree of certainty: "Nietzsche is dead, signed God."

What did Friedrich Nietzsche, the nineteenth century German philosopher (1844-1900), actually mean when, in Book Three of *The Gay Science*, he declared that "God is Dead"? Not only that, but: "All of us are his murderers":

> Have you not heard of that madman who lit a lantern in the bright morning hours, ran to the market-place, and cried incessantly: "I am looking for God! I am looking for God!" As many of those who did not believe in God were standing together there, he excited considerable laughter. "Have you lost Him, then"? said one. "Did he lose His way like a child"? said another. "Or is He hiding? Is He afraid of us? Has He gone on a voyage? or emigrated"? Thus they shouted and laughed. The madman sprang into their midst and pierced them with his glances.
>
> "Where has God gone"? he cried. "I shall tell you. **We have killed Him — you and I. We are His murderers.** But how have we done this? How were we able to drink up the sea? Who gave us the sponge to wipe away the entire horizon? What did we do

when we unchained the earth from its sun? Whither is it moving now? Whither are we moving now? Away from all suns? Are we not perpetually falling? Backward, sideward, forward, in all directions? Is there any up or down left? Are we not straying as through an infinite nothing? Do we not feel the breath of empty space? Has it not become colder? Is it not more and more night coming on all the time? Must not lanterns be lit in the morning? Do we not hear anything yet of the noise of the gravediggers who are burying God? Do we not smell anything yet of God's decomposition? Gods too decompose. **God is dead. God remains dead. And we have killed Him.** How shall we, murderers of all murderers, console ourselves? That which was the holiest and mightiest of all that the world has yet possessed has bled to death under our knives. Who will wipe this blood off us? With what water could we purify ourselves? What festivals of atonement, what sacred games shall we need to invent? Is not the greatness of this deed too great for us? Must we not ourselves become gods simply to be worthy of it? There has never been a greater deed; and whosoever shall be born after us — for the sake of this deed he shall be part of a higher history than all history hitherto."

Here the madman fell silent and again regarded his listeners; and they too were silent and stared at him in astonishment. At last he threw his lantern to the ground, and it broke and went out. "I have come too early," he said then; "my time has not come yet. The tremendous event is still on its way, still travelling — it has not yet reached the ears of men. Lightning and thunder require time, the light of the stars requires time, deeds require time even after they are done, before they can be seen and heard. This deed is still more distant from them than the distant stars — and yet they have done it themselves."

It has been further related that on that same day the madman entered churches and there sang a requiem. Led out and quieted, he is said to have retorted each time: "What are these churches now if they are not the tombs and sepulchres of God"?

Nietzsche's assertion that "God is Dead" is not simply a metaphysical statement. He did not come up with the definitive argument to prove beyond all reasonable doubt that God could not possibly exist, except in the minds of human beings. For Nietzsche, the "Death of God" theory refers to the complete loss of belief in accepted religious world-views, along with the system of values they uphold, in particular their moral values. The "Death of God" announces the advent of the age of nihilism, an age of cultural sterility arising from this abandonment of faith, which may well end in catastrophe as far as any truly human existence is concerned. "God is Dead" theology is the Siamese twin of atheism.

Nietzsche asserts that God is dead in the hearts of modern men and women — killed by rationalism and science. He seems to be suggesting that the acceptance of the "Death of God" will also involve the ending of accepted standards of morality and purpose, without which society is threatened by a nihilistic situation where people's lives are not constrained by ethical considerations, or guided by any faith-related sense of purpose.

For Richard Rubenstein (see page 131), the catastrophe that could very well prove Nietzsche's point is the Holocaust, and the murder of six million Jews, one-and-a-half million children among them. For certain, such a tragedy would shake the foundations of any person's belief in God. It is clear that in the Holocaust all standards of morality broke down, and faith in God was rendered meaningless. When published in 1966, *After Auschwitz* created great controversy as "Death of God" theology:

> Rubenstein virtually invented Holocaust theology. He argued that Jews (and Christians) who accept the traditional belief that God has chosen Israel and acts providentially in history must either interpret the Holocaust as Divine punishment or as the most radical challenge ever to traditional belief (from the back cover of *After Auschwitz*).

And yet, we hear that even secular Jews went to their deaths reciting the most sacred words within Judaism: "Hear O' Israel, the Lord our God, the Lord is One" (*Deuteronomy* 6:4). This affirmation of faith in God must have provided some measure of comfort, much in the same way that reading *Psalms* comforted me over the last few months. Within Judaism there is something known as *Responsa Literature*,[1] a series of ritual and moral questions and answers great sages dealt with throughout the centuries. This was also the case with the Holocaust. Rabbi Ephraim Oshry (1914-2003), a *Talmudic* authority who survived the ghetto of Kovno, Lithuania, wrote a five-volume work, *Responsa from the Holocaust*, in which he responds to a multitude of questions relating to Jewish observance, practice and behavior actually posed during that era of horror. The community he served were Jews whose belief was not shattered despite the mass murder that engulfed the Jews of Europe. However, it is interesting to note that Oshry primarily dealt with questions of ritual concern, rarely touching upon issues of moral import, knowing that it is virtually impossible to understand God's role in the Holocaust on a moral level.

The sad reality is that, depending on the circumstances, any one of us could claim that "God is dead." Elie Wiesel heard himself pronounce it when that angel-eyed boy was hanging on the gallows in Auschwitz. My parents said it when their twelve-year old daughter was killed by that trolley-car. My friend said it when his daughter was born with cerebral palsy. And, I uttered it when I first became fatally ill: "God is dead." These words are chilling and

---

1. Known in Hebrew as *Sh'eilot U'teshuvit* ("questions and answers"), *Responsa Literature* constitutes a special class of rabbinic literature — commentaries devoted to the exegesis of the Bible, the *Mishnah*, the *Talmud* and the codes of Jewish law. The codes themselves contain the rules for ordinary incidents of life. The *Responsa Literature* covers all these topics and more. Many of the questions were theoretical in nature, since they requested information concerning all departments of knowledge. Accordingly it contains rulings on practical Jewish laws and customs., which include ethics, business practices, philosophy of religion, astronomy, mathematics, history and geography.

fierce, because human nature is such that we all want to believe in something beyond ourselves. We do not dwell on such a belief every moment of our lives, or perhaps even sporadically. Whether one's faith is a psychological crutch, a "figment of the imagination" or a genuine belief, a person does not want to hear that his or her last resort for help has been stripped away.

"God is Dead" theology is a most painful one. But, even if God is not dead, for us mortals, any sense that God has taken an extended vacation is virtually the equivalent. In a human being's hour of need, philosophical questions of Free Will versus Determinism play little role. We want answers; and, while we do not expect direct Divine intervention, we do hope to be consoled. However, when we are witness to so much collective and individual suffering in our immediate world, our intuitive reaction is to wonder not only "where God is," but also "if God exists." Abraham Joshua Heschel wrote *God in Search of Man*. At this very moment, I, like many others in my same situation, am engaged "in search of God."

Are We All Basically Agnostics?

Lying here, motionless, feels not so different from having a liver CAT scan. When undergoing one, I always felt that I was being placed in a time machine. I would enter that claustrophobic "back-to-the-future" time tunnel and, for approximately an hour-and-a-half, I would lie absolutely immobile. I imagined that death would be like an eternal MRI. To pass the time, I would begin singing to myself, then move on to talking to myself, even telling jokes to myself, and finally talking to God. It never failed. For that relatively short time that my body was being scanned, I would ponder the wonders of the universe. How did "it" all begin? "Who" could have thought of such a "thing"? The "it" and the "thing" were the world and human beings. The "Who" was God. But, the why of the "it," the why of the "thing" and the why of the "Who," I didn't know. Just as all those hot-shot medical experts could not figure out what was wrong with my liver until it was too late, I could not figure what God was all about until it was too late. I have no idea why the Almighty decided to create us. Just as I sometimes believed in my doctors, yet often did not, so too did I sometimes believe in God, but oftentimes did not.

The main reason I could not conclude that God existed or not, which basically would define me as an agnostic, was the way the Bible begins, as cited beforehand:

In the beginning, God created the heaven and the earth. Now,
the earth was unformed and void, and there was a darkness
upon the deep, and the spirit of God was hovering over the
waters (*Genesis* 1:1-2).

If "in the beginning" there was God, how could there already have
been "darkness"? If God is the First, how could there have been
anything before Him or Her? According to Rashi (see page 98) the
Hebrew prefix which is attached to the word "beginning" should
not be translated as "in the," but rather as "when," i.e.: "When God
began creating the 'cycle' of the heaven and earth, God had already
created darkness." It is not at all clear that such a grammatical
nuance actually helps. The very idea that the Bible, which is, among
many things, a definitive biography of God, would begin with such
theological confusion is enough to make someone a devout
agnostic, a term which strikes me as an oxymoron. How can one be
an ardent agnostic; that is, a fervent believer in that which one does
not know? It is one thing to admit that I know what I don't know, (it
is always wise to acknowledge that we do not know the answers to
certain questions), but it is quite another matter to assert belief in
that which we do not know. This borders on nihilism — believing
fervently in nothing.

Agnosticism is a concept, not a religion. It is a belief related to
the existence or non-existence of God. An agnostic is a person who
feels that God's existence can neither be proved nor disproved on
the basis of current evidence. Agnostics note that some theologians
and philosophers have tried to prove, for millennia, that God exists.
Others have attempted to prove that God does not exist. Neither
side has convincingly succeeded at its task.

While the eighteenth century French author and playwright,
Francois Voltaire (1694-1778) is often considered the father of
agnosticism, the term "agnostic" was coined in 1869 by Thomas H.
Huxley (1825-1895), a well known English religious skeptic. He

combined "a," which implies negative, with *"gnostic,"* which is a Greek word meaning "knowledge." Huxley wrote:

> When I reached intellectual maturity, and began to ask myself whether I was an atheist, a theist, or a pantheist; a materialist or an idealist; a Christian or a freethinker, I found that the more I learned and reflected, the less ready was the answer; until at last I came to the conclusion that I had no part of any of these denominations, except the last... So, I took thought, and invented what I conceived to be the appropriate title of "agnostic." It came into my head as suggestively antithetic to the "gnostic" of Church history, who professed to know so much about the very things of which I was ignorant...

Robert G. Ingersoll (1833-1899) is perhaps the most famous American agnostic of the nineteenth century. He commented on the problem of theodicy (the defense of God's goodness and omnipotence in view of the existence of evil):

> There is no subject — and can be none — concerning which any human being is under any obligation to believe without evidence... The man who, without prejudice, reads and understands the Old and New Testaments will cease to be an orthodox Christian. The intelligent man who investigates the religion of any country without fear and without prejudice will not and cannot be a believer... He who cannot harmonize the cruelties of the Bible with the goodness of Jehovah, cannot harmonize the cruelties of Nature with the goodness and wisdom of a supposed Deity. He will find it impossible to account for pestilence and famine, for earthquake and storm, for slavery, for the triumph of the strong over the weak, for the countless victories of injustice. He will find it impossible to account for martyrs — for the burning of the good, the noble, the loving, by the ignorant, the malicious, and the infamous.

There are different categories of agnostics: agnostic theists — those who believe that a deity probably exists; agnostic atheists — those who believe that it is very improbable that a deity exists; empirical agnostics — those who believe that God may exist, but that little or nothing can be known about Him/Her/It/Them; agnostic humanists — those who are undecided about the existence of God. All these agnostics do not really consider the question to be particularly important. They have derived their moral and behavioral codes from secular considerations. Their ethical behavior would not be altered if God were proven to exist.

Of course, the most controversial agnostic is the man who challenged the creation of human beings as recorded in the Bible — Charles Darwin (1809-1882), the father of the Theory of Evolution. His notion that we are descended from the apes was considered by fundamental religionists as a threat to the idea that God was the Creator. In his book, *Life and Letters,* he wrote:

> The mystery of the beginning of all things is insoluble by us; and, I for one must be content to remain an agnostic.

Could it be that the agnostic has it right: The truth of the existence or non-existence of God is inherently unknowable. We can have scientific or real knowledge of phenomena, but when it comes to what lies behind such phenomena, all metaphysical discourse cannot provide sufficient evidence that entitles any of us either to deny or affirm anything, which is to say: **Belief is not based on fact, but rather faith**. But, faith in what, and in whom? It cannot be, as Ingersoll suggests, a faith in the traditional God of biblical history — there are just too many stories in the Old and New Testaments involving God that can only be defined as anti-human; that is, anti-God's creations. And yet — not knowing? It sounds too defeatist for me.

*Evolution and Creation:
Why the Conflict?*

Five-year-old-child: Mommy, where did I come from?

Mother: Well, Jimmy, one day, your Daddy and I said to each
other that we wanted to have a baby. So, after we talked
about it for some time, we agreed that we would try. We
went to bed one night, and cuddled real close to one another.
Daddy kissed me and I kissed Daddy. Then Daddy got on top
of Mommy. Do you understand so far, Jimmy?

Child: Mommy, Billy comes from Boston. I want to know:
Where did I come from?

Everyone wants to know where he or she came from. It
would be nice if we could settle for the simple answer of comedian
Shelly Berman. When he was acting the role of a child psychologist,
inviting questions from the audience, one person asked: "Doctor,
where do babies really come from"? Berman, not missing a comedic
beat, replied: "If your child asks you this question, 'where do babies
come from', we've had some success with pointing"!

There are many theories about the origin of the human species:
creation as recorded in the Old Testament, evolution, Big Bang
happenstance, molecular division. The question is: Are these
theories mutually exclusive? Does the acceptance of any one of the
latter three necessarily negate the existence of God, as recorded in

the biblical account of the Creation? Do they contradict the creation of man and woman as described in *Genesis*?

The conflict between two basically different philosophies of the beginning of the world was sharply and dramatically brought into focus in the famous Scopes "Monkey Trial" in 1925 in the state of Tennessee. It has been referred to as the "trial of the century," as it pitted science against religion and dealt with separation of "church and state." According to Tennessee law at that time, it was forbidden to teach the Theory of Evolution. John T. Scopes, a twenty-five year old science teacher and football coach in Dayton, Tennessee, nevertheless introduced the idea of evolution to his students. Threatened with suspension for his "heretical" views, the evolutionist wanted to challenge the law, and invited Clarence Darrow (1857-1938), the famous defense lawyer, not only to defend Scopes, but also to put the notion of biblical creation on trial, and to show that rational thought and scientific advancement must be included in the teaching of the origins of the human species. The prosecuting attorney was William Jennings Bryan (1860-1925), three-time candidate for the presidency of the United States, and secretary of state under President Woodrow Wilson.

Facing a prejudicial judge and jury at the Rhea County Court House, Darrow chose to put Bryan on the stand. Being refused the right to call upon scientists to support his argument for evolution, Darrow decided that he would disprove Bryan and the Bible. It turned the tide of the trial, and of public sentiment.

> **Darrow**: You have given considerable study to the Bible, haven't you, Mr. Bryan?
>
> **Bryan**: Yes I have, I have studied the Bible for about 50 years.
>
> **Darrow**: Do you claim that everything in the Bible should be literally interpreted?
>
> **Bryan**: I believe everything in the Bible should be accepted as it is given there.

Darrow: Do you believe Joshua made the sun stand still?

Bryan: I believe what the Bible says.

Darrow: I suppose you mean that the earth stood still?

Bryan: I don't know. I am talking about the Bible now. I accept the Bible absolutely.

Darrow: You believe the story of the flood to be a literal interpretation?

Bryan: Yes, sir.

Darrow: When was that flood?

Bryan: I would not attempt to fix the day. I never made a calculation.

Darrrow: What do you think?

Bryan: I do not think about things I don't think about.

Darrow: Do you think about the things you do think about?

Bryan: Well, sometimes.

Darrow: You believe that all the living things that were not contained in the ark were destroyed?

Bryan: I think the fish may have lived.

Darrow: Don't you know there are any number of civilizations that are traced back to more than five thousand years?

Bryan: I am not satisfied with any evidence I have seen.

Darrow: You believe that every civilization on the earth and every living thing, except possibly the fishes, were wiped out by the flood?

Bryan: At that time.

Darrow: You have never had any interest in the age of the various races and peoples and civilizations and animals that exist upon the earth today?

Bryan: I have never felt a great deal of interest in the effort that has been made to dispute the Bible by the speculations of men or the investigations of men.

Darrow: Don't you know that the ancient civilizations of China are six thousand or seven thousand years old, at the very least?

Bryan: No, but they would not run back beyond the Creation, according to the Bible, six thousand years.

Darrow: You have never in all your life made any attempt to find out about the other peoples of the earth — how old their civilizations are, how long they have existed on the earth — have you?

Bryan: No, sir, I have been so well satisfied with the Christian religion that I have spent no time trying to find arguments against it. I have all the information I want to live by and to die by.

Darrow: Do you think the earth was made in six days?

Bryan: Not six days of twenty-four hours.

Darrow: Did you ever discover where Cain got his wife?

Bryan: No sir; I leave the agnostics to hunt for her.

Darrow: Do you think the sun was made on the fourth day?

Bryan: Yes.

Darrow: And they had evening and morning without the sun?

Bryan: I am simply saying it is a period.

Darrow: The Creation might have been going on for a very long time?

Bryan: It might have continued for millions of years.

Despite his devastating cross-examination of Bryan, Darrow made little dent in the armor of the earth creationists, as they are called. Like Bryan, they believe in a literal interpretation of the Bible — that the earth and its current life forms, as well as the rest of the universe, were created by God, approximately six thousand years ago. There are variations of the earth creationists that try to harmonize their traditionalist thinking with science. Some believe that the world may indeed be billions of years old; however, God still created the earth and the rest of the universe. There are some whom we might call theistic evolutionists, who believe in the Theory of Evolution, but claim that evolution was a tool created, employed, determined and controlled by God. While the fundamentalist Judeo-Christian view of the Creation is basically supportive of the biblical account of the world's beginning, Hinduism teaches that there are a number of creation stories, and Buddhism teaches that creation occurs repeatedly throughout time.

But, given Darrow's presentation, which was dramatized on stage in the play, *Inherit the Wind* (1955), by Jerome Lawrence and Robert E. Lee, and later made into a movie by the same title (1960), starring Spencer Tracy as Clarence Darrow and Frederic March as William Jennings Bryan, belief in the evolution of the species is hard to resist. With his 1859 publication of *On the Origin of the Species*, Charles Darwin presented a cogent argument for evolution, which was fought by religious fundamentalists with unrelenting zeal.

Yet, in spite of fundamentalist insistence on the literal veracity of Scripture, there are many religious stalwarts who accept *Genesis'* account of Creation as a metaphor. According to *Genesis*, the world was created in six days, Adam lived nine hundred and thirty years (5:5), and Noah was six hundred years old when the flood occurred (7:6). We can take these figures literally, or we can surmise that biblical time-reckoning is measured on a metaphorical scale. This allows the account of the Creation as recorded in *Genesis* to agree with observed evolution.

Clarence Darrow said:

> Science gets to the end of its knowledge and, in effect, says, "I do not know what I do not know," and keeps on searching. Religion gets to the end of its knowledge, and in effect, says, "I know what I do not know," and stops searching.

There is only partial truth in this statement. Many religionists continually examine and reexamine their belief system in light of technological developments and social changes. Religion need not necessarily remain stagnant, as Darrow would suggest.

As a matter of consistency, evolutionists must assume that we are not the ultimate descendants of a prior species, the perfection of a progression that began with a lesser form of humankind. There must be some consideration that we are a link on the road to an even higher and more refined form of human existence. Indeed, given the evil machinations of the human mind that saw its ultimate expression in the person of Adolf Hitler, it is hard to imagine that we have reached the pinnacle of our development.

As noted previously, the two accounts of the creation of the first man and woman by God should be sufficient to cast serious doubts about the immutability of the "origin of the species" as set down in the Bible, unless we understand the creation of man and woman as a metaphor. The story of Adam and Eve in the Garden of Eden might possibly have taken place thousands of years after the beginning of God's universe, and was introduced for reasons that have nothing at all to do with the Creation. They are part of a creation legend, wherein we learn that already at the very beginning of time there were moral dilemmas of great magnitude that had to be faced; and, how we stand up to various tests that are placed before us, whether by accident or design, will determine if we fall from grace or not.

In short, evolution may challenge the historical authenticity of the stories of Adam, Eve, Cain and Abel, but it does not and cannot diminish their allegorical significance, which introduces issues of ethical importance. Further, no one should think that when the Old and New Testaments trace the events of the ancient Hebrews and early Christians, there is no historical veracity to them. For certain, evolution does not contradict unfolding dramas that include as their lead actors such personages as Moses, Joshua, David, Solomon, Jesus and Paul. Their stage presence, or presence at that stage in history, was part of the ongoing evolution of human beings as individuals capable of thinking and acting.

While I have said before that, like many people, I seek simple answers, especially to complicated questions, the truth is that I cannot rest because I am not satisfied with seemingly facile answers, such as: "my time was up," or, "it was fate," or "I had it coming to me for reasons I will never understand," or "I didn't take good care of myself," or "I did not go to synagogue and pray to God regularly." The more I try to understand why I am about to die relatively young, the more I become irritated by any responses that strike me as glib. Blind faith evades the question of why tragic things happen to decent people. Religious fervor is too simple a nostrum to truly help one contend with one of life's ultimate questions: Why me?

Evolution, with all its attraction (although I do find it pretty revolting to think that my ancestors may have been chimpanzees), does not seem to help in one's search for meaning in death. While rational thought may lead one to believe in evolution or any other scientific (and non-theistic) view of the creation of the world, it leaves me cold. Why? Because, we human beings are not just made up of matter and mind, as Descartes would have us believe. We are a race of passion and emotion that needs to be nourished by something beyond Kant's worlds of "pure and practical reason."

I can provide the reader with countless objective reasons as to why I love my wife and children, but ultimately it is not reason that makes me happy when they are happy, or sad when they are sad, or pained when they are pained. Such empathy is driven by passion, by my emotional composition.

Belief in the Theory of Evolution does not "turn me on." It lacks passion and emotion, those two feelings that pump the heart with excitement. *On the Origin of the Species* lacks literary flare. The Bible, with its simple account of Creation, yet with its complex set of problems, brims with dramatic anticipation. I cannot address questions to some bacteria or ape-like creature from which evolutionists believe life began. But, I can address God, as did my ancestors, Abraham and Moses to name a couple. If God did create the world as described in the Bible, then what, in God's name, has happened over the centuries? No monkey or molecule can answer that for me.

The Theory of Evolution does not provide me with the emotional outlet that I so desperately need to help me understand what is happening to me. I find no solace in adopting Darwin as my God, just as I would find little comfort were I to embrace atheism, agnosticism or "God is Dead" theology as my personal ideology. This is not to say that evolutionists, atheists or agnostics cannot be persons of emotion or passion (despite my earlier observation that outwardly atheists seem rather grim) — it's the message that primarily lacks sensation. By process of elimination, it seems that I am left with a traditional acceptance of God, which includes a metaphorical as well as an historical depiction of Him or Her, as outlined in the biblical rendition of the Creation. As such, this understanding of the biblical origin of human beings does not have to contradict evolutionist theory. So, I guess I can have my Divine cake and eat it, all the while continuing to pester the Creator in my eternal search for answers about life and death.

Is Materialism Our New God?

A couple in Long Island, New York, was embroiled in a bitter litigation with the Village Council of Southampton over the violation of the township's building code. The couple set out to build the most expensive house in the history of New York, a twenty-five million dollar castle by the sea, with sixty-three rooms, gothic towers and a thirty-foot waterfall cascading into an indoor pool. Among the medieval decorations in this palace was one suit of armor, purchased for over three million dollars. The home, which many would call a true monstrosity, was fittingly named "Dragon Head."At the opposite end of the spectrum, there is the story of a father who was so busy earning a buck, that he was away on a business trip when his wife gave birth. Returning home, he rushed into the bedroom where his newborn child was sleeping, and remarked: "What a beautiful crib. And to think it only cost $99.50"! In the words of French novelist, Honore de Balzac (1791-1850): "Materialism is a recipe for pure madness."

We are told by that eternal pessimist, *Ecclesiastes*: "He who loves money will never be content" (5:10). I question the accuracy of such a generalization. I certainly was not a rich person, but I may have been wiser in putting my faith in the stock market than in God. What is the ultimate inheritance that I wish to leave to my children that can be measured — belief in God, moral integrity, family unity?

For certain, all these will aid them; but, the money I leave them to ease their lives is something tangible. After all, it will not be the goodwill of God that will pay for my funeral, and it will not be God's generosity that will provide a sufficient income for my wife.

The Beatles are correct, "money can't buy me love," but it can buy peace of mind; and, peace of mind is the primal psychological state we should try to attain during our lifetimes, without which we will be unable to "rest in peace" or incapable of finding "eternal peace" when the time comes. I imagine that eternal peace is far preferable to eternal agitation and annoyance. While it is still unclear whether I will merit a measure of immortality, it is clear that my financial savings have bought me that much needed "peace of mind," as I know that my monetary inheritance will leave my family comfortable.

Many of us live in a world of exaggerated avarice and materialism (especially if one considers the gulf between industrial nations and third world countries). One could argue that if the same effort to earn money were invested into finding out about God's existence, there might be fewer religious skeptics in the world. But, since the rewards of monetary endeavors are immediate, whereas the payback for Divine investments is tangential at best, what is so terribly wrong with building a "golden calf" once in a while? The problem is that the "golden calf" becomes the end, and not the means to the end.

What could be a better example of this than the medieval period in Europe, when the Catholic church built cathedrals, monuments of gold, on the backs of the masses. It could very well be that the religious architects felt they were paying homage to God by creating something that was aesthetically conducive to spiritual enhancement, but the extravagance was so enormous that the church building itself became the object of deification. In fact, the magnificence of some of the churches was so overwhelming and awe-inspiring that the onlooker felt humbled. The question is, rather than feeling humbled, did he or she feel humiliated, because the poorest of the poor were expected to give what little they possessed to the erection of these palatial sanctuaries? Such exploitation cannot be a saintly attribute. Clearly, there is an "edifice complex" at work here, the church and the church fathers virtually replacing Divine attention.

It is difficult to understand this opulence, considering the proscription in the Ten Commandments against the fashioning of "graven images" of God. Is the artistic beauty of the Notre Dame's stained-glass windows in Paris, the architectural wonder of Antonio Gaudi's La Safrada Familia in Barcelona, the awesome splendor of the Sistine Chapel in the Vatican in Rome a true reflection of the type of church that God wanted worshipers to pray in? As stunningly magnificent as are these holy places, it is easy to become cynical about religion when one confronts such luxury and ostentation. Imagine what might have been done with the wealth poured into these shrines, had it been directed toward the eradication of disease or hunger.

It is the rejection of the notion that the "meek shall inherit the earth" that places materialism in the first pew. The modest and humble individual is rarely the one who rules the world. And so, a thirst for power and riches takes over. Greed replaces humility and self-indulgence replaces modesty. But, just as money can purify the bastard, so too can it bastardize the pure. Prestige has become so important, it would seem that only wealth can secure a place at the social table. This is often the case, for it is usually the wealthy lay-members who occupy positions of influence within their religious institutions. The "meek" inherit the last pew in the church or synagogue.

It would appear that there is a material ethic in America. How else does one explain the millions of dollars poured into the state lotteries? Then again, a monetary quick-fix, remote as it might be, is more easily attainable than a sudden inoculation of a Divine serum. After all, religious experience takes time to cultivate. One can feel the crunch of a dollar in one's hand, but can never be sure of God's touch. The music industry's sex icon, Madonna, recorded the famous pop song, *Material Girl*: "We are living in a material world, and I am a material girl." (Perennially, the most popular TV programs in the United States are ones like *For Love of Money* and *The Millionaire*.) And, most significantly, the legal tender of the United States has become a religious symbol. U.S. dollar bills bear the legend: "In God we trust." Is this not a charge to adopt materialism as a new deity? Why shouldn't we place our faith in the "**Almighty** buck"?

So, why is it that, as satisfied as I am that I am leaving behind a measure of financial security for my family, I am still restless? It is true, you can't take your money to the grave, although many of the ancient Egyptian potentates were buried with all their wealth, indeed many were encased in their gold. But, what good did that do for the young Tutankhamen? I guess I am looking for something that is more durable than material possessions, that can help me understand life's mysteries. Money can come and go, the stock market can rise and fall. Putting one's faith in something so transient, although necessary for basic survival, cannot provide answers to questions pertaining to matters of right and wrong, of good and bad, of life and death. Such an attitude led to the downfall of Willy Loman, the tragic protagonist of Arthur Miller's signature play, *Death of a Salesman*, as he committed suicide, clinging to the vain hope that the $20,000 from his life insurance policy, which would be left to his sons, would compensate for his failure to instill within them a sense of moral direction.

True, money can sometimes buy one's way out of an impending tragedy. Oskar Schindler literally bought "his Jews" to save them from certain death at the hands of the Nazis. Wealth can purchase expensive medicines that may prolong life. The pain of old age can be eased, if the best personal and institutional care can be procured.

But riches, money and possessions cannot buy answers to existential questions, such as why sickness strikes arbitrarily, and why aging has to be accompanied by memory loss or physical disabilities.

The notion that we can "buy time" only works up to a point. Ultimately, my economic well-being did not prepare me for my early departure from this world. To understand the nature of the universe, the wonders of the world, the life cycle of the human species and the emotions of the human heart, one must move beyond worshipping a silver dollar. While I would like tangible answers to my never-ending quest to comprehend the magnitude and reason for our existence on this planet, I know that it cannot be done by placing faith in a fleeting, and frankly selfish and simple answer, such as materialism.

Are There Other Gods – Political Ideologies, Flag, Anthem and Country?

Throughout my many years of political activism, I often found myself wedded to a particular political ideology that eventually disappointed me. I suspect this is true for many people who have adopted a variety of political philosophies. While the ideal form of socialism and communism is most compelling, their limitations on freedom of expression turned out to be terribly repressive. It also became apparent that communism, which has as its goal the subjugation of individual ideological biases, was incapable of suppressing the natural human desire to believe in something beyond a single and total loyalty to the state as an end in itself. The breakdown of the Russian empire is a clear indication that the absolute demand for faith in one's country and a singular political dogma simply does not work — even when maintained by force and oppression.

What may be true of totalitarian regimes may affect democracies as well. Democracy can be cynically exploited to prefer the majority view, with little regard for minority dissent. All forms of government, of whatever stripe, create a dynamic of their own that must be maintained through a sense of patriotism, which is fueled by national symbols. All of this makes good sense except when these symbols become an end in themselves: the Hammer and Sickle, the Stars and Stripes, the Swastika (no intention here to equate the symbols). It should also be noted that religious symbols, which are supposed to provide a ritual passage to God, can become objects of worship themselves.

In the United States, the constant struggle to keep church (religion) and state separate is precisely because the mixture of religion and nationalism is a dangerous combination. The fusion of the two can result in a chauvinistic theology in which the national ego is projected onto God, and Divine blessing is seen to be bestowed exclusively upon one country over another. Most certainly, in the Arab world, where Islam is the state religion, an exaggerated expression of patriotism is fostered, which can whip up a frenzy where perceived threats to the state, seen as an attack upon Islam and Moslems, are treated with scorn, hostility and violence. In Israel, an atmosphere of religious fanaticism amongst a small segment of the population, whose adherents confuse religiosity with nationalism, brought about the assassination of Prime Minister Yitzhak Rabin (1922-1995). Indeed, history is dotted with such interaction of religion and nationalism — from the time of the Crusades (and before) to the Salem witch trials in 1692. When the majority religion becomes the state's religion, it is virtually impossible to distinguish between the state and God. The strength of the religious right in America produces a "Jesus Day" in Texas, which is a clear violation of church and state.

Since September 11, 2001, when the World Trade Center was destroyed by terrorists, a phenomenon has taken hold in America. In churches and synagogues throughout the United States, the singing of patriotic songs during religious services has become standard procedure. Rare is the prayer gathering that does not include an emotional rendition of God Bless America.

One must be continually vigilant, for any "rally-round-the-flag" sentiment can lead to an extremism that is difficult to control. For example, the jingoistic mantra of "America the Great" that was heralded with such pride after the bombing of the Twin Towers, may create a much needed harmony in a country that is so culturally diverse as is Uncle Sam, but it also can set the stage for unchecked hatred, accompanied by populist demands for responses to terrorism that could be unnecessarily devastating. And, speaking of Uncle Sam, with that imposing face and that finger pointing directly at us, sternly saying, "I want you," has all the trappings of the standard sketch of God that any grade school kid might draw: God with that long white beard, summoning us to "His Call."

What is that clarion call? For Americans to envelop themselves in the Stars and Stripes and not to criticize government policy, especially in light of terror; for to do so could be considered traitorous. The intention to play on one's most basic fears in order to stir up a patriotic zeal seems to facilitate the ruling power's appetite for instituting severe limits on civil liberties in the "pursuit of justice." Who will be those suspected of undermining justice? Arab-Americans, because they look the part. It begins here, but it can lead to those who are openly critical of government policy. They will suffer, because putting an American flag in one's window and singing *America the Beautiful* in synagogues and churches represents total unity to carry out actions — any actions — to protect the United States.

National unity and pride in one's country are a necessity. Given the scale and scope of the terrorist attacks in New York and at the Pentagon in Washington, DC, and, while American boys are engaged in combat, such an outpouring of identity with national symbols is to be expected. But, it cannot be exploited to the extent that the state reaches worshipful proportions. It is a very slippery slope, as national fervor can run amok. Singing the national anthem of "bombs bursting in air" in houses of worship crosses that delicate and thin line that separates religion and nationalism. In the defense of freedom (or rather in the name of "national security"), one must not confuse, and ultimately put on an equal footing, God, flag and country, the three-fold banner of national unity, in order to wage a war on terrorism that could limit domestic freedoms, release bigotry, curtail open debate, violate moral standards of behavior (even in wartime), censor the press, trample human rights and punish the wrong people for the crimes of Osama bin Laden and company.

What can readily turn a state into an object of pseudo-Divine adulation is the threat to its physical survival and economic viability. Basic liberties are the first aspects of any democracy sacrificed in such a case. We all know what havoc absolute allegiance to the state, which brings with it a blind faith in its leaders, can wreak upon a nation and the world. Indeed, if one takes Stalin's Russia, Mussolini's Italy, Franco's Spain and Hitler's Germany, and more recently, Hussein's Iraq, Amin's Uganda, Pol Pot and Son Sann of the Khmer Rouge's Cambodia, Milosevic's Yugoslavia, the blind faith in these gods of "ideological purity" led to disaster.

So I have come to rule out absolute political ideologies, national anthems, flag and country as my religion. A state that assumes God-like magnitude usually derives its power from a people who have been stirred to passionate belief in "my country — right or wrong," or have succumbed to unbridled oppression and fear. They confuse morality with obedience, rarely refusing to carry out a clearly immoral order. The administrators of these Divine estates are politicians, either elected or imposed — flesh and blood mortals, some, like those listed above, who have abused their Divine Spark.

So, if one were to ask why do I believe in God? I would ask in return, how can one deify the state — elevating its leaders to Divine proportions? Given what we know about countries and their leaders, better to put one's trust and faith in God than in human beings.

Question #31 *Does God Have a Special Relationship with the Jewish People and the Land of Israel?*

> Blessed are you O' Lord, who has chosen His people Israel out of love.
>
> Blessed are you O' Lord, who loves His people Israel.
>
> Blessed are you O' Lord, our God, King of the universe, who has chosen us among the nations of the world.

It should be made clear that in raising this Question, along with the next one, **Is God a Zionist?** (see page 131, footnote 1), I am relating to matters of Jewish belief and concerns. This is not to say that the role Israel plays in Christianity is of no significance, but the focus here is on the perceived relationship between God and the Jewish people and the Land of Israel as a matter of Jewish theology. As one who lives in Israel, these two questions obviously are critical for me. If the answer to these two questions is "yes," then my *Aliya* (in Hebrew — ascension, also immigration to Israel) was incredibly justified. A positive answer would have a powerful impact on the ultimate meaning of my life, as I will have chosen a geographical locale where God truly is with me, and thus be able to breathe a theological sigh of relief.

If one scans the Jewish prayer book, one would find that Israel is a focal point of the Jews' spiritual longing: 1) "Gather us up from the four corners of the world and bring us back to Your land [Israel]"; 2) "Out of Zion shall go the *Torah* and the word of Lord from Jerusalem"; 3) "Lead us upright into our land [Israel]." Indeed, Israel comes in a close second to God in the amount of attention afforded to it in the prayers.

> May You shine a new light upon Zion, and may we all speedily merit its light. Blessed are You, O' Lord, who fashions the luminaries.

This blessing, which introduces the morning prayers, captures the spirit of the creation of the world, and God's powers within the natural order of the universe. The prayer addresses the fashioning of light as the first order of God's creative business.

A straightforward understanding of this prayer can be quite problematic for a believing Jew who resides outside of "Zion." For Jews living in Cleveland or St. Louis, Paris or London, Johannesburg or Buenos Aires, Kiev or Moscow, the notion of Jerusalem and Israel as the centers of God's attention must be quite unsettling, particularly when the prayer connotes physical movement toward Israel. But, it is difficult to argue against the premise that Jewish theology and history clearly point to a special relationship between God and the Jewish people and the Land of Israel.

The above blessing, which introduces the morning prayers, serves as a convincing theological statement: The relationship between God and the people of Israel primarily finds its commanding place within Jewish religious belief in a historical context — the concept of a "Chosen People." As the nascent stages of Jewish history unfold, we read in *Exodus* how Jewish identity was forged on the anvil of the Egyptian experience of slavery. It is against this background of disenfranchisement that the Jews eventually become a nation, charged with becoming a "kingdom of priests and a holy nation" (Exodus 19:6). This is the dramatic moment referred to in the biblical narrative:

> Now, therefore, if you will listen to My voice and keep My commandments, then you will be my **treasure** among all the peoples... (*Exodus* 19:5); For you are a holy people unto the Lord, your God, and the Lord has **chosen** you to be His **treasure** out of all the peoples on the face of the earth (*Deuteronomy* 14:2).

This concept of "chosenness," a subject of perennial controversy among Jews (as well as non-Jews), is understood to mean that Israel has been selected — chosen — for a particular mission: To bring to the world a Divine message of a decent humanity. This concept is interpreted by most modern Jewish thinkers as an obligation to implement God's demand of fulfilling moral and ritual commandments, rather than an attempt to ascribe privilege or superiority of any sort to the Jews.

What is the problem here? It is fairly obvious that the testing ground for this "chosenness" to go into effect is in the Land of Israel, for the commandments were given to the Israelites on their way to the "Promised Land," promised to Abraham, who was told:

> Go forth from your native land, the land where you were born, from your father's house to a land that I will show you. I will make you a great nation, and I will bless you; and I will make your name great, and you shall be a blessing. I will bless those who bless you and curse those who would curse you; and all the families of the earth shall bless themselves by you (*Genesis* 12:1-3).

In the Sinai, the Israelites were charged with a Divine dictate, that once they arrived in that land promised to Abraham, they were to build a society based on the rejection of the abuse of power as exercised by the pharaohs of Egypt, one that would be founded on a prophetic vision of social justice and equality.

It becomes clear that the idea of "chosenness" is attached to a particular land — Israel. Only in a self-contained and self-defined Jewish state do Jews have both the authority and responsibility for all its social, political, cultural, economic, religious, educational and military decisions. It is only in Israel that Jews can put to the test those Divine precepts of justice and equality demanded of them in that Sinaitic somewhere of Jewish experience, as they journeyed to the Promised Land to establish an independent nation.

Does this mean that the only place for Jews to collectively fulfill that Divine mandate of creating a God-like world, a utopian society, paradigmatic for the world, is in Israel? It would certainly seem so, which leads to the most disturbing question of all for a believing Jew who lives outside of Israel — Is God a Zionist?

Is God a Zionist?

Is God a Zionist? If one were to talk to Orthodox settlers in the West Bank, then their answer would be "yes." Otherwise, how can one explain their zealotry, their willingness to face incredible danger, living as they do, as a minority among a couple of million Palestinians?

But, even here there is a conflict of Orthodox Zionist views. For many believing Jews (and non-Jews), Israel represents the biblical promise of a Divine redemption that will usher in the Messiah. In Israel, two very different theologies crowd the Orthodox mind. One claims that Israel can only be redeemed with the advent of the Messiah, while the other holds that the Messiah will only arrive after Israel redeems itself. In the Israeli reality, such a contradictory national/theological approach still supports the idea that Zionism is intimately entwined with God.

Zionism, as is generally conceded, is not a new concept. Political Zionism, Cultural Zionism, Labor Zionism, Revisionist Zionism are indeed outgrowths of the modern political world — answers to the continued estrangement and persecution of the Jewish people, primarily in Eastern Europe during the mid-nineteenth century, and later in Western Europe in the years leading up to and during World War II. However, Spiritual Zionism is as old as the Jewish exile of 70 B.C.E., when the Jews were driven out of ancient Israel by the Romans.

From that moment on, Jews faced Israel and prayed three times a day for a return to Zion, invoking God's name. Perhaps, most telling is a prayer recited after a meal. During the weekday, a Jew begins this prayer by reciting *Psalms* 137:

> By the waters of Babylon, there we sat, there we wept, as we remembered Zion. There, on the poplars, we hung up our lyres, for our captors asked us there for songs, our tormentors, for amusement, "Sing us one of the songs of Zion." How can we sing a song of the Lord on alien soil? If I forget, you, O Jerusalem, let my right hand wither; let my tongue stick to my palate if I cease to think of you, if I do not keep Jerusalem in memory at my happiest hour (1-6).

This longing for a return to Zion, expressed already at the first Jewish exile in 586 B.C.E. with the plundering of Jerusalem by the Babylonians serves as a metaphor for exile. Yet, on the Sabbath, the dream of return is realized, and a Jew recites as an introduction to the grace after meals *Psalms* 126:

> When the Lord restores the fortunes of Zion — we see it as in a dream — our mouths shall be filled with laughter, our tongues with songs and joy. Then shall they say among the nations, "The Lord has done great things for them!" The Lord will do great things for us and we shall rejoice. Restore our fortunes, O' Lord, like the watercourses in the Negev. They who sow in tears shall reap with songs of joy. Though he goes along weeping, carrying the seed-bag, he shall come back with songs of joy, carrying his sheaves (1-6).

This theme of Divine Zionist intervention is further manifested at the close of the same grace after meals. Again, in metaphorical exile — during the weekday — a Jew says: "God Who makes great the salvations of His king." On the Sabbath — in the metaphorical return to Zion — a Jew says: "God who is a tower of salvations of His king." What is the subtle difference here? Again it is grammar at its theological best. The Hebrew word for "makes great" and "tower" are based on the same root word. During the week, when we are in "exile," we are striving to "make things great" so that we reach the pinnacle of our fulfillment, the "tower" (the "greatness"), which stands firmly in Zion. The following words then merge together:

> God Who does kindness for His anointed, to David and his descendants forever. God Who makes peace in the heavens, may He make peace upon us and all of Israel.

The very fact that David's name is invoked here, the first king of Israel, surely indicates that the never-ending struggle of the Jewish people to fulfill its dream of return to a Promised Land by eventually establishing a Third Jewish Commonwealth after two thousand years of statelessness is based on a belief in a Zionist God. Indeed, such a belief has inspired the Jews to fend off Babylonians, Romans, Crusaders, Inquisitors, Cossacks, Tzars, Nazis, Arabs and terrorists. This Divine Zionism has established the Jews as possessing the longest living national liberation movement in human history.

What is the original source of that dream of return? It is found in the story of Jacob's name change to Israel (see page 98). This name change is concretized in the opening prayer in the morning liturgy, when a Jew says:

> How good are your tents O' Jacob, Your dwelling-places O' Israel (Numbers 24:5).

The interpretation of this seemingly simple phrase is that our initial status is one of a transitory nature. Like Jacob, in our youth, we are often wily, sometimes deceitful. There is an impermanence in our personality, just as there is something temporary about a tent. As we mature, we move into a home, something permanent. Most significant is that the Hebrew word for "dwelling-place" is *Shechina*, which refers to God's Divine presence that was centered in the Ark of the Temple in ancient Jerusalem. This biblical quote comprises the first words a Jew utters when entering the synagogue to join in collective prayer. From that very moment, it is incumbent upon the worshipper to pray that he or she will move from a transient stage of Jacob (Diaspora) to an enduring stage of Israel, where the Almighty's Divine presence dwells.

Is God a Zionist? The most perfunctory examination of Jewish history would suggest that the answer is "yes." So, how do those Jews who live in the Diaspora deal with such a powerful theological concept? The answer seems almost self-evident, as outlined in the previous question in its discussion of the prayer, "May You [God] shine a new light upon Zion." If, as that prayer suggests, the glow of the Creation shines brightest on Israel, one would assume the closer one is to the light of the Creation, the closer one is to God.

Can Empiricism Prove God's Existence?

The basic idea behind empiricism is that all knowledge is based on experience, that knowledge can be derived through careful observation and cataloging of phenomena and extrapolating laws or principles from these observations. Empiricism is not only employed as a philosophical response to theological questions, but also is a means to explain all phenomena, such as in the field of medicine, which bases most of its knowledge on empirical observation of the causes and courses of diseases.

The philosophy opposed to empiricism is rationalism, represented by such thinkers as Descartes and Spinoza. Rationalists assert that the mind is capable of recognizing reality by means of reason, a faculty that exists independent of experience. Immanuel Kant attempted a compromise between empiricism and rationalism. He agreed with the empiricists by attributing to the mind a function that incorporates sensations into the structure of experience. He also agreed with the rationalists in claiming that this structure could be known *a priori*, without resorting to empirical methods.

For the most part, empiricism has taken on a flexible meaning, and is used in connection with any philosophical system that finds all of its materials in experience. The term "empirical laws" is applied to those laws that express relationships observed to exist among phenomena, without implying the explanation or cause of the phenomena.

For Judaism, of all the philosophical approaches employed to make sense of a religious belief in God, empiricism is most suitable. Why do I say this? Because Jewish religious belief is based on the historical drama of the Jewish people from its earliest stages until the present.

> Moses received the *Torah* from Sinai and delivered it to Joshua, and Joshua to the Elders, and the Elders to the Prophets, and the Prophets delivered it to the men of the Great Synagogue... (*Mishnah — Sayings of the Fathers* 1:1).

In Judaism, the *Torah* leads to interpretation by the *Talmud,* which in turn is divided into sub-sections of *halachic* (legal) and *aggadic* (fable) understandings, which are further dissected by rabbinic commentators, and ultimately codified in a mini-legal code — the *Shulchan Aruch.*[1]

For a Jew, the ultimate proof of God's existence is found in the prayer book and given expression three times daily.

> Blessed are You O' Lord, our God, and God of our ancestors, God of Abraham, God of Isaac, God of Jacob. The great, mighty and awesome God — the supreme God, Who bestows beneficial kindness and creates [owns] everything. Who remembers the righteousness of the fathers and brings a redeemer [or redemption] to their children's children, for the Creator's sake, with love. Ruler, Helper, Savior and Shield,

---

1. A compendium of those areas of Jewish religious law that are applicable today. The *Shulchan Aruch* ("Set Table") was composed by Rabbi Yosef Karo (1488-1575) of Safed, Israel in the 1560s, and became generally accepted as authoritative after Rabbi Moshe Isserlis (1530-1572) of Cracow, Poland supplemented it in the 1570s with notes (known as the *Mappah* — "Tablecloth") giving the rulings followed by *Ashkenazic* (Eastern European) Jews. It is the most widely current code of Jewish law in practice, covering all areas of one's life.

Blessed are You, O' Lord, the shield of Abraham (from the
Sh'moneh Esrei).

What is most interesting here is that the prayer stresses a personal
relationship between God and each of the three patriarchs. The
prayer could have been far more efficient had it been written: "God
of Abraham, Isaac and Jacob." This individual emphasis tells us that
we too can forge an intimate "I and Thou" relationship with God as
articulated by Jewish theologian, Martin Buber (1878-1965), in his
powerful book, *I and Thou*. That one's offspring's offspring is
included is a certain indication of generational continuity and
obligation. This "passing on" of religious understanding that took
wing at Sinai is reinforced when we recite:

> You shall love the Lord, your God, with all your heart, with all your
> soul and with all your might. Let these matters that I command
> you today be upon your heart. **Teach them diligently to your**
> **children** ... I am the Lord, your God, Who brought you out of
> Egypt to be a God to you. I am the Lord, your God (*Deuteronomy*
> 6:5-7; *Numbers* 15:41).

Jews have empirical proof of God's existence in the experiences of
their Jewish forebears. Jews are commanded: "In every generation,
a Jew is obligated to see him- or herself as if he or she has gone out
of Egypt" (from the *Passover Hagaddah*). None of those who guided
the Jewish people throughout history wavered from their belief in
the God that the previous generations believed in.

If belief in God has withstood the ongoing simultaneously
glorious and tortuous historical drama of the Jewish people, **who**
am I to *question* the existence of God? For a Jew, the answer to the
ultimate question — **"who is God"?** — is: God is the God of
Abraham, Isaac, Jacob, Joseph, Moses, Joshua, the Rulers of Israel,
the Prophets, the Elders; the God Who created the world and
fashioned human beings; the God Who gave identity to the Jewish
people while wandering in the desert, transitioning from slavery to

freedom; the God of all the children who have been instructed in His or Her ways as it is commanded: "Teach them diligently to your children" (*Deuteronomy* 6:7). These few words have become the watchword of the Jewish faith-heritage, and which Jews have recited every day for centuries without interruption, which means, ultimately: God is the God of all generations, of our generation.

Is God "in the Details"?

Albert Einstein said: "I want to know how God created this world. I am not interested in this or that phenomenon, in the spectrum of this or that element. I want to know His thoughts... the rest are details." Not having the cerebral capability of Einstein, or even approximating his genius, understanding how God created the world is simply beyond my intellectual abilities. Therefore, I will have to settle for "details." It could just be that I will find God "in [those] details."

It has been posited that the Oslo Accords (1993) failed in forging an ultimate peace agreement between Israelis and Palestinians because they were drafted with broad strokes, and not fine print. The details were not carefully worked out. I would not be plagued with doubts about God if I just concentrated on the large picture: God created the universe. But, once I go beyond that, I get bogged down. I can't get any details that will solidify my belief. I keep coming back to the same question over and over again: Why did God create a world that is so filled with natural disasters and human evil? If I could only figure out what is the relationship between God and us, I would not have to leave my commitment to faith in God only at the door of the creation of the world.

Could it be that after the creation of the universe, God dropped out of sight? If so, why do we continually beseech the Almighty?

What is it that we expect from God — comfort, guidance, forgiveness, sustenance?

The children of Israel are wandering in the desert. Unsure of what awaits them, they begin to doubt the wisdom of following God's chief advocate, Moses. They consider that it might have been better to have remained in Egypt. At least, though enslaved, they knew what to expect. The uncertainty of trekking through the wilderness of Sinai created unbearable anxiety, despite the promise of becoming a great nation, chosen by God, not for privilege, but for obligation, to become a "light unto the nations" (*Isaiah* 42:6). While Moses is making his way up Mount Sinai to receive the *Torah*, the people, influenced by their surroundings, build a "golden calf,"[1] worshipping a new god, because they sought something that was tangible.

Suddenly, there is thunder and lightning, and "a resonant, well-modulated voice" echoes throughout the Sinai expanse: "Hear, O' Israel." The Israelites are stunned and drop to their knees and cry out: "The Lord, our God, the Lord is One." As noted before, the prime theological foundation of Judaism is expressed in the words: "Hear, O' Israel, the Lord our God, the Lord is One" (*Deuteronomy* 6:4). In the prayer book, this religious affirmation of belief in one God is sandwiched between a prayer of love: "Blessed are You, O' Lord, Who chooses His people Israel out of love," and then afterwards, the continuation of the Deuteronomic quote: "And you shall love the Lord, your God, with all your heart, with all your soul

---

1. An object of worship among the ancient Hebrews, mention of which occurs principally in *Exodus* 32:1-4: "When the people saw that Moses was so long in coming down from the mountain, the people gathered against Aaron [Moses' brother] and said to him, 'Come, make us a god who shall go before us, for that Moses, who brought us from the land of Egypt — we do not know what has happened to him.' ... Thus he [Aaron] took from them [gold earrings] and cast in a mold, and made it into a molten calf [golden calf]." Most writers have accepted the view that the worship of golden calves was borrowed from the Egyptians, supported by the fact that Aaron sojourned in Egypt shortly before constructing such an idol.

and with all your might" (6:5). In that one moment of high drama, the Jewish people created a religion that at its very core was a dialogue, a partnership between God and the people, enwrapped in supplications of love.

This partnership, this dialogue between God and the people of Israel, is a paradigm for all relations, not only Divine, but also human. Balladeer Perry Como's (1912-2001) insistence that "love makes the world go round" is Divinely inspired. Our relationship with God is supposed to be based on mutual love, and thus should serve as an example of the relationship between husband and wife, parent and child, siblings, friends, nations. How we express that love and maintain its flame is in the **details** of everyday living. God has set the course for us, but we must provide the fine-tuning.

If this is the case, why are the very first familial relationships in the Bible so dysfunctional? **The proof is in the details. So, let us explore those details**. Could it be possible that God is using us as straw men and women to prove a point? Have we gone straight for the dessert, skipping the cocktail, the hors d'oeuvres, the soup, the antipasti and the entrée?

❖　❖　❖

ACT I — Scene 1:

What is the scenario? God creates the world, populating it with human beings. The Creator places choices before His or Her creatures, trying to divine whether they will act in good faith and behave in a way that will be appreciative of the gift of life bestowed upon them though doing absolutely nothing to merit it. This "give and take" begins in the allegorical Garden of Eden. Almost immediately the notion of consequences for one's behavior and actions are introduced. Satan, in the form of a snake, tempts Eve to eat from the "tree of knowledge of good and bad." Falling under the serpent's spell, she is virtually hypnotized into doing that which was forbidden by her Creator.

> When the woman saw that the tree was good for eating and a delight to the eyes, and that the tree was desirable as a source of wisdom, she took of its fruit, and ate. She also gave some to her husband, and he ate (*Genesis* 3:6).

As a result of this act of disobedience, Eve, Adam and the serpent are punished throughout the generations.

ACT I — Scene 2:

The brothers Cain and Abel now enter center stage — and murderous jealousy characterizes their story, with Cain being banished to the east of Eden for the murder of Abel, destined to be a wanderer, marked for life with an "x" on his forehead, so that whoever he comes in contact with will know of his deadly crime.

ACT I — Scene 3:

Once the generations of Adam and Eve pass away, Noah and his family appear on the biblical arena. But, his generation does not live up to Divine standards, as frivolity, greed and self-indulgence rule the day. And so, a flood is brought down upon the world, from which only Noah and his family, as well as pairs of animals, are saved in order that God can begin the world anew.

First Interregnum:

At this point, God makes the decision not to destroy the human race again on account of one generation's evil behavior. God concedes that He or She may have started the world off on the wrong foot. God had begun with the universal human being, Adam. The Creator worked backwards, going from the universal to the particular, and had obviously failed. So, in order to drive a Divine point across to us human beings, God decides to start over again with the particular — with the details — and move to the universal.

ACT II — Scene 1:

God tries a new approach at creating a social order that would be respectful and law-abiding. According to the biblical narrative, the next major personality to appear on the scene is Abraham. Abraham is not a universal figure, but a particular individual — a Jew. But, even here, with Abraham and the two subsequent patriarchs, his son and grandson, Isaac and Jacob, we see failure to adhere to the highest moral standards. It culminates in the dastardly act of Jacob's sons, who leave their brother Joseph, of whom they are insanely jealous, in a well so that he would either die or be captured by the Ishmaelites. Once again, God has experienced failure, as even the particular individuals who were Divinely chosen for leadership could not live a Divinely moral life.

ACT II — Scene 2:

It is at this point that Moses comes forward, that great leader who saw God "face to face." The Hebrews are now in Egypt, being treated with benign neglect, as Joseph, sold to the Egyptians, has risen within Pharaoh's court, and been accorded a modicum of respect. But, a new king arose in Egypt who did not know Joseph; and, fearful that the Hebrews are multiplying in such force that they will overwhelm the Egyptian population, he gives the order to kill all the first-born males among them. Therefore, upon Moses' birth, his mother hides him for three months, and then sets him afloat in the Nile river, watching from the bulrushes what will become of him. A daughter of Pharaoh takes him out of the wicker basket in which he had been placed and presents him to Pharaoh as if he is her own.

The plot now moves at a quickened pace:

> Some time after that, when Moses had grown up, he was sent out to his kinfolk and witnessed their toil. He saw an Egyptian beating a Hebrew, one of his kinsmen. He turned this way and that and, seeing no one about, he struck down the Egyptian and hid him in the sand. When he went out the next day, he found two Hebrew slaves fighting; so he said to the offender: "Why do you strike your fellow"? He retorted: "Who made you chief and ruler over us? Do you mean to kill me as you killed the Egyptian"? Moses was frightened, and thought: Then the deed is known! When Pharaoh learned of the matter, he sought to kill Moses; but Moses fled from Pharaoh. He arrived in the land of Midian, and sat down beside a well.
>
> Now the priest of Midian had seven daughters. They came to draw water, and filled the troughs to water their father's flock; but shepherds came and drove them off. Moses rose to their defense, and he watered the flock. When they returned to their father Reuel, he said: "How is it that you have come back so soon today"? They answered: "An Egyptian rescued us from the shepherds; he drew water for us and watered the flock." He said to his daughters: "Where is he then? Why did you leave the man? Ask him in to break bread." Moses consented to stay with the man, and he gave Moses his daughter Zipporah as his wife. She bore a son whom he named Gershom [the Hebrew meaning of the name is "stranger there"], for he said: "I have been a stranger in a foreign land" (*Exodus* 2:11-22).

Having no way of knowing that he was a Hebrew, Moses seems to have identified with the slaves, and intuitively understands the evil of ruling over a people subject to bondage. On three occasions, Moses becomes incensed at acts of social injustice. When a non-Jew abuses a Jew, he kills the offender; when a Jew abuses a Jew, he intercedes; and when non-Jews harass other non-Jews, he drives the reprobates off.

Eventually, Moses returns to Egypt to lead his people out of slavery, but, even with all his greatness, with his moral conscience driving him to stand up for what is right and decent, his behavior falls short of the highest moral standards. Eventually, he is punished, deprived of entering into the Promised Land, allowed only to glimpse it from a distance. (Here it is debatable whether the punishment fit the crime: Moses had only tried to extract water from a stone by hitting it with a stick.) In the meantime, the people whom he had led out of slavery behave in an ungrateful fashion — always complaining and moaning about the conditions of desert life: the housing, the food, the social life. They seem hopelessly lost and begin to rebel against Moses' leadership — fighting among themselves.

ACT II — Scene 3:

It would seem that, at this juncture, God is fed up and summons Moses to ascend Mount Sinai in order to dictate to him some rules. It becomes clear that Divine intuition, granted to Adam and Eve, and passed on through the ages to the generation of Moses, is not sufficient to fashion moral standards by which societies can function with stability, decency and constancy. So, that which should have been intuited had to be literally engraved in stone; thus, we have the *Torah*.

ACT II — Scene 4:

No sooner were the Divine laws of moral behavior delineated in "detail," than they were broken almost systematically. The Bible produces two more major personalities: David and Solomon, kings of Israel. David's conquest of the land of Canaan is so brutal that he is prevented from establishing Jerusalem as the capital of the new Israelite kingdom, with the Temple as its centerpiece. The bloodshed he causes to the Jebusites in taking their land is followed by a personal transgression, when, in his sexual thirst for the beautiful Batsheva, he orders her husband, Uriah, to the front lines of battle where he is sure to be killed, so that he, David, can take her for his own.

"The apple does not fall far from the tree." David's son, Solomon, builds the Temple, expands his kingdom, adorns the sanctuary with foreign elements, and eventually, as a result of his colonialist hunger for power, sets the stage for a breakdown of the kingdom into two: Israel and Judah.

The prohibitions against murder, adultery, jealousy, coveting that which is your neighbor's — all moral laws set in stone as the Ten Commandments, without which a society cannot function — are violated by David and Solomon. From then on, the moral and physical demise of the Israelites is not far behind. After two relatively brief periods of sovereign rule, the Jews enter into a prolonged era of dispersion. Even the prophets who rail against moral turpitude, are often scorned, their warnings disregarded and belittled.

Second Interregnum:

Recognizing that neither Divine intuition nor Divine intervention in the form of a written document could lead God's creatures to act in ways that were morally just, God, according to Christian theology, turned to the most celebrated religious figure in human history, Jesus, to set things straight. And, while Christ's influence on human behavior is felt today by millions of Christians around the world, in his time, he was ridiculed greatly as he tried to bring a message of God to the people — a message of moral uprightness, inclusive of a "turn the other cheek" philosophy. His failure was seen in his crucifixion, where, according to Christian theology, he died for the sins of humankind.

ACT III — Scene 1:

It is at this juncture that God may have thrown up His or Her proverbial hands, admitting defeat. The mantle was passed on to us humans, and we became not just God's interlocutors but so self-important that we replaced God. Recognizing that what was written in the Bible was not sufficient to guide the human race, some well-schooled rabbis in the Galilee of ancient Israel and later in Babylonia, at the beginning of the Common Era, composed two major religious-legal works, the *Mishnah* and the *Talmud*,[1] which in minute detail expounded on the laws of the *Torah*, leaving no room for doubt as to how one should behave. It was the rabbis, and only the rabbis, who would be the sole interpreters and arbiters of God's intentions.

So total was the control of the rabbinical hierarchy, that if someone testified in a court of law as to why he (at that time women were not permitted to testify) had acted in a specific way, claiming that "the voice of God" instructed him to do so, the testimony would be considered inadmissible. Understandably, we cannot have every individual bring as justification for certain behaviors a Divine dictate; in fact this is often the case, as historically, so much of human action has purportedly been performed in the name of God. Yet, the power of the rabbis, which seems to be regarded as an almost natural inheritance by many of today's clergy who see themselves as Divine stand-ins, has left God back in the wilderness of Sinai.

(It is significant that the *Haggadah* — the "telling" in Hebrew — which recounts the story of the exodus from Egypt, and which is

---

1. Traditional Jews believe that the *Talmud*, which contains the *Mishnah*, was given at the same time as was the *Torah* — to Moses at the top of Mount Sinai.

read once a year during the Jewish holiday of *Passover*, does not mention Moses by name. It seems terribly unfair, as he was the dominant personality of that time. The reason is that no one should elevate him or herself to a position of Divine supremacy, for such elevation can wreak havoc. It can be dangerous to "play God.")

❖   ❖   ❖

Could it be that the allegorical and historical narratives of the Old and New Testaments were exclusively designed only to teach moral lessons? Could it be that God's involvement in our world is no more than that of Divine instructor, guide, teacher? Could it be that God has given us all the tools to lead a life of righteousness, leaving it up to us to make proper use of them? Could it be that the failures of many of our mythical and historical heroes — Adam, Eve, Noah, Abraham, Moses, David, Solomon — are so meticulously drawn in order to emphasize that the contravention of God's many particular social and ethical dictates will lead to dire consequences? Could it be that we have driven God from our world?

Is it at all possible that if we not only believed in the moral "details" of the ancient religious narratives, but also acted upon them, the world would be a better place? There is the story of someone who came to the Buddha, and asked him: "Where is God"? The Buddha thrust the man's head into a pool of water, holding it there while the man battled furiously to get air. When the Buddha finally released his grip, the man, gasping and choking, asked: "Why did you do this"? The Buddha replied: "When you want to find God as much as you wanted to breathe, you will find the Almighty."

Nothing is achieved without effort. Wisdom is not acquired overnight. One does not become a nuclear physicist in an instant. Hard work is the prerequisite for knowledge. No one reaches the end of a journey without following a long and arduous path. Just as a child builds a vocabulary by learning new words one by one, storing them up so that sentences flow, in order that ideas and thoughts can be articulated and communicated, so too must we explore all possibilities in our search for proof of God's existence. Instead of just looking at the headline, we need to read "the story behind the story"; that is, to read between the biblical lines, for it is just possible that it is there — **in the details** — we will find God.

Can God Perform Miracles?

(A third grader comes home from religious school.)

Mother: What did you learn today?

Kid: Nothing. Something about Moses and the Red Sea.

Mother: Well, tell me what the teacher said.

Kid: No big deal. I want to go play outside now.

Mother: Not until you tell me what the teacher taught you.

Kid: Okay. The Jews were running away from the Egyptians when they got to this huge sea. They then took some wood, bricks and chains, and built a huge bridge. They quickly ran over the bridge to the other side. And when the Egyptians came after them and were on top of the bridge, the Jews blew it up, and all the Egyptians drowned.

Mother *(Aghast)*: Is that what your teacher told you?

Kid: No. But, if I told you what she told me, you'd never believe me.

In Judaism, the Yiddish proverb, "a Jew cannot live without miracles," is most applicable. The question that looms large is whether we should attribute miracles to the work of God or to our own steadfastness and, whether the difference matters.

No one is above using the word miracle to describe what he or she considers are extraordinary events, such as the wonders of nature: the change of leaves in the autumn, a rainbow, the birth of a child. Other expressions of miracles include: "It is a miracle that I found you"; "what a miracle that we survived that storm"; "it is absolutely miraculous that she is alive after what she has been through." And, in reference to the questions of God's relationship to the Jewish people, Israel and Zionism: "The reestablishment of Israel after two thousand years of dispersion is a modern-day miracle."

Yet, we all know that each one of the above miracles can give way to some sort of scientific or historical explanation. (To understand some of the scientific explanations would be a miracle to me, as I am still awed by electricity, convinced it falls into the category of an inexplicable wonder, as it is beyond my comprehension.) By definition, a miracle is that which cannot be explained. The American folk-singing group the Weavers sang these lyrics: "The Virgin Mary had a baby boy." How is that possible? Oh, I know, it's a miracle, and by definition a miracle is "inconceivable," beyond explanation by reference to currently believed notions of the regularities of nature. Therefore, one either believes the miracle of the Virgin Birth or does not.

So what does one do with Jesus? Let us say that we believe the miracle that Jesus walked on water, what and where does that get us? Does anyone truly believe that we would ever be able to walk on water. We would drown if we were to try. To be sure, if we believe that Jesus walked on water in his day, are we then to believe he could perform acts of a miraculous nature today?

"A miracle cannot prove what is impossible but is necessary to confirm what is possible" (Maimonides, *Guide to the Perplexed*, 3:24). It is only natural to wish for a miracle when we are in trouble or when we are sick; or to a lesser degree, to succeed in a job or to do well in school. "In times of expectation, one must rely on a miracle" (*Talmud Yebamot* 39b). The very notion that a human being can attain what seems impossible is a driving force behind many people's aspirations. There is no better example of this than the story of Helen Keller (1880-1968) and her devoted teacher, Ann Sullivan (1866-1966), immortalized in *The Miracle Worker* (1959) — an apt title for the wondrous movie describing the story of blind, deaf-mute Ms. Keller's life and Ms. Sullivan's heroic part in her achievements. Again, the question looms, were Helen Keller's accomplishments an act of Divine interference or of human determination?

Despite all my rational instincts, I find it difficult to reject the efficacy of miracles and their inexplicable wonder. While we are cautioned to "not rely on miracles happening daily" (*Talmud Shabbat* 32a), thereby trying to absolve ourselves from being active partners in shaping our own lives and the lives of those around us, the belief in "a miracle… is necessary to confirm what is possible" — what we might ultimately achieve.

One cannot comprehend a miraculous event by any manner of logic. Also, because of the very definition of miracles, one cannot pick and choose them. It is all or nothing – with the exception of the miracle of the Creation. It is all a matter of faith. However, even now, given modern technology, when everything is verified by either CNN or the Internet, it is a **miracle** if we believe in the **miracle** of the Creation. There was no one there to either film it or post it on a website.

So what do we do with Judaism's emphasis on the miraculous ways of God: Noah's ark, the parting of the Red Sea, the burning bush, to name but a few? Indeed, the entire developing drama of the Jewish people as played out in the *Torah* is based on the supernatural interference of God. A Jew could say that the giving of the Ten Commandments, which fashioned the social agenda for the Jewish people for generations to come, was the greatest of all miracles. All these occurrences defy logic. In the same manner that Jews reject Christian miracles (the Virgin Birth, Jesus' walk on the water, the resurrection of Christ), so too would they have to deny their own. How do we find a way out of this seemingly troubling and contradictory dilemma? Could it be that all these "supernatural" events can indeed be explained either scientifically or allegorically or naturally?

It is not so simple. It strikes me that all miracles, whether one seeks an explanation through Divinity, science or human will, derive from one miracle that fits the traditional definition of a miracle — that which is beyond any human calculation, reason or understanding, that is beyond definition — the miracle of the Creation, which is renewed every time we witness the birth of a child. No one will ever be able to comprehend this one — no matter how many Big Bang theories scientists come up with. A Jew recognizes this when reciting the first prayer in the morning: "I thank you God... that You have returned my very breath to me." Jews should consider every day that they are alive a miracle, looking at themselves in the morning as a continuation of the miracle of the Creation. Such an approach to life elevates one's worth as an individual and heightens sensitivities and appreciation for the people with whom a person interacts and for the things and events which he or she encounters.

It is this notion of miracles that brings me to the brink of believing in God, even as I question God's role in the universe and our daily lives. As I finish my pen-ultimate question, believing in miracles can fortify me, as I contemplate what might lie in store for me.

Is There an Afterlife, Heaven and Hell, a Soul?

"If a man dies, shall he live again"? (*Job* 14:14).

This question has intrigued the human mind from ancient times to our day. Questions of what happens at one's death have hung over the heads of humankind as long as humanity has existed. When people are gripped by the fear of death, they are enslaved in cruel and unforgiving bondage.

Being at the "gateway to heaven," I have decided to save the question of a possible "afterlife" for last. For Jews, the notion of an afterlife is tied into Jewish eschatology — that apocalyptic moment when there will be an end to the agony of history, and when a new era of bliss for humanity at large will be ushered in. This will be led by a Messiah who will bring peace among the nations, with the Jewish people living in their land under their own sovereignty, unencumbered by persecution and anti-Semitism.

This is all foreseen in the prophecy of the "Valley of the Dry Bones":

> And the hand of the Lord came upon me, taking me out by the Holy Spirit and set me down in the valley. It was full of bones. I was led all around them; there were many of them spread over the entire valley, and they were very dry. And God said to me, "O mortal, can these bones live again"? I replied, "O' Lord God, only You know." And God said to me, "Prophesy over these bones, and say to them: O' dry bones, hear the word of the Lord! Thus

said the Lord to these bones: I will cause breath to enter you and you shall live again. I will lay sinews upon you and cover you with flesh, and form skin over you. And I will put breath into you, and you shall live again. And you shall know that I am the Lord." I prophesied as I was commanded. And while I was prophesying, suddenly there was a sound of rattling, and the bones came together, bone to matching bone. I looked, and there were sinews on them, and flesh had grown, and skin formed over them; but there was no breath in them. Then God said to me, "Prophesy to the breath, prophesy, O' mortal! Say to the breath: Thus said the Lord God: Come. O' breath, from the four winds, and breathe into the slain, that they may live again." I prophesied as God commanded me. The breath entered them, and they came to life and stood on their feet, a vast multitude (*Ezekiel* 37:1-10).

These mesmerizing words of God, spoken through Ezekiel, are music to my ears. (By the way, one of the reasons that I have ruled out cremation is that I want to keep my options open, just in case Ezekiel's prophecy comes true.) What about the resurrection of Christ? I wonder whether there would be any chance that I could rise up to heaven like Jesus. Okay, I'm Jewish, but Jesus considered himself a Jew. I would love to follow in his footsteps, even if his resurrection was marked by extreme brevity. Would such a possibility be dependent on my believing in Jesus Christ? If yes, do I have the emotional will to forfeit my Jewish faith for Christian belief? And, should I not take the risk, being unable to believe in the resurrection story, what about as a substitute something akin to that story of the "Valley of the Dry Bones"?

It is virtually impossible for me to believe that, after death, I will get up and walk right out of the grave. Then again, what if do, and God puts the wrong sinews or flesh on me? Suppose I come back to life as a flabby-looking Cass Elliot (of the singing group *The Mamas and the Papas*) or a muscular-looking Muhammad Ali in his prime. My family would never believe that it's really me. Suppose I come back to life and find my wife remarried!

Again, to those believers who can buy into such theories of re-embodiment, I tip my hat. However, I would ask them: Why would God force people to go through the pain of dying, only to be revived at a later date?

In traditional Jewish sources, the afterlife is called the *olam habah*, the World to Come. However, a similar term is also used to refer to a renewed utopian *olam hat'chyiah*, the World of Resurrection — a place where the body and soul are reunited to live eternally in a truly perfected state. For Yaakov Astor, author of *Soul Searching: Seeking Scientific Foundation for the Jewish Tradition of an Afterlife*, such a World will only come into being after the Messiah appears, and will be initiated by an event known as the "Great Day of Judgment." This newly constituted World is the ultimate reward, a place where the body becomes eternal and spiritual, while the soul becomes even more so.

According to Astor's theory, the *olam habah* is the place righteous souls reside after death. That place is sometimes referred to as the World of Souls. It is a place where souls exist in a disembodied state, enjoying the pleasures of closeness to God. Thus, genuine near-death experiences are presumably glimpses into the World of Souls, the place most people think of when the term "afterlife" is mentioned.

We read in the *Zohar:*[1]

All souls are subject to reincarnation; and people do not know

---

1. Meaning "splendor," the *Zohar* is the central work of the *Kabbalah* and is a commentary on the *Torah*. The *Zohar* first appeared in Spain in the thirteenth century, and was published by a Jewish writer named Moses ben Shem-Tov de Leon. He ascribed this work to a rabbi of the second century, Simeon ben Yohai. Written in medieval Aramaic and medieval Hebrew, it contains a mystical discussion of the nature of God, the origin and structure of the universe, the nature of souls, sin, redemption, good and evil, and related topics. The *Zohar* is not one book, but a group of books. These books include scriptural interpretations as well as material on theosophic theology, mythical cosmogony, mystical psychology, and what some would call anthropology.

the ways of the Holy One, blessed be He! They do not know that they are brought before the tribunal both before they enter into this world and after they leave it; they are ignorant of the many reincarnations and secret works they have to undergo, and of the number of naked souls, and how many naked spirits roam about in the other world without being able to enter within the veil of the King's Palace. Men do not know how the souls revolve like a stone that is thrown from a sling. But the time is at hand when these mysteries will be disclosed. (*Zohar* II 99b)

The *Zohar* and related literature are filled with references to reincarnation, addressing such questions as: Which body is resurrected and what happens to those bodies that did not achieve final perfection; how many chances a soul is given to achieve completion through reincarnation; whether a husband and wife can reincarnate together; if a delay in burial can affect reincarnation; and if a soul can reincarnate into an animal.

Sefer HaBahir[1] used reincarnation to address the classic question of theodicy — why "bad things happen to good people," and vice versa:

Why is there a righteous person to whom good things happen, while [another] righteous person has bad things happen to him? This is because the (latter) righteous person did bad in a previous [life], and is now experiencing the consequences... What is this like? A person planted a vineyard and hoped to grow [sweet] grapes, but instead, sour grapes grew. He saw that his planting and harvest were not successful, so he tore it out. He cleaned out the sour grape vines and planted again. When he saw that his planting was not successful, he tore it up and planted it again. (*Bahir* 195).

---

1. Meaning "the book of clarity," *Sefer HaBahir* is the earliest work of Jewish mystical literature, traditionally attributed to the first century Nehunya ben HaKanah. It first appeared in the twelfth century in Provence, but incorporates ancient texts, which had been transmitted to Europe from the East. Written in Hebrew and Aramaic, the style of this short book is obscure.

Job lends credibility to this idea of multiple lives. It is one of the texts the mystics like to cite as a scriptural allusion to the principle of reincarnation:

> Behold, all these things does God do — twice, even three times with a man — to bring his soul back from the pit that he may be enlightened with the light of the living (33:29-30).

In other words, God will allow a person to come back to the "world of the living" from the "world of the dead"[1] a second, a third or a multitude of times.

My father used to tell me, when he was already in his nineties: "If you can't remember something, then forget it"! Let us assume that I have reached death's door at an early stage in my life because I led an unrighteous life in a pervious "reincarnation." Well, I would like to remember that previous life and what exactly I did that was so condemnable. Only through recollection will I be able to know how, when my next reincarnation comes around, to right my previous wrongs.

❖ ❖ ❖

I would like to establish if there really is a heaven and a hell. Most religions teach that good people go to some sort of paradise, usually heaven, after they die. Heaven is characterized as a place of unsurpassable happiness — the ultimate utopia. It is commonly taught and believed that all who go there will live joyfully ever after. Yet, considering what a wonderful place it is supposed to be, no one I know seems to be in a hurry to get there. The exception might be those Islamic "Jihadists" who perpetrate suicide bombings to gain a place in heaven along with seventy virgins. Of course, if entrance into heaven is supposed to be a reward for the good deeds a person

---

1. The "world of the dead" is one of the classic biblical terms for *Gehinnom* or "Purgatory."

does here on earth, needless to say, conventional wisdom and pure logic would condemn those Jihadists to hell.

Death, which according to most traditional beliefs is the gateway to heaven, is generally viewed as something to be avoided at all costs. Through medical science we usually do everything we can to prevent death as long as possible. If such a journey to heaven could be by means of some Heavenly express, would we not find the trains empty? Do not most people prefer the continuation of their present life here on earth to any immediate possibility of taking up residence in heaven?

Perhaps the reason for the reluctance to enter the hereafter through death is that no one has ever provided us with a truly convincing prediction as to what is in store for the righteous once they arrive in heaven. If we are to spend all eternity there, why does God not give us a hint about what to expect? Will we spend our time plucking harps? Will we sit and simply gaze adoringly upon God? These are only two possibilities of what might happen in heaven. Can anyone imagine doing either for eternity? Eternity is, after all, a long time! British historian and author Paul Johnson put it this way:

> Heaven ... lacks genuine incentive. Indeed, it lacks definition of any kind. It is the great hole in theology (*The Quest for God*).

❖ ❖ ❖

But, heaven isn't the only problem we run into when we consider popular views of life after death. What about the unrighteous, those who don't measure up? What happens to them? Are they consigned to hell? For those who believe that the wicked will burn forever in Purgatory, we need to ask a simple question: Would a merciful God inflict excruciating pain and torment on human beings for millions and millions of years — throughout all eternity? Could the great Creator of the universe be so unfeeling and uncaring? No matter what sins I may have committed over the years — wittingly and unwittingly — will I be transferred to a permanent home of burning coals? I was always led to believe that God is all-forgiving, and even the worst sinner is subject to exoneration — a sort of Divine pardon. (In the Bible, the original Hebrew word used for hell is *Sheol*, but it primarily refers to the grave, the place where everyone, whether good or evil, goes when they die. *Sheol* is mentioned in the Old Testament sixty-five times.)

And what happens to all the hapless people who die so terribly young, whose personalities are not fully formed, like the one-and-a-half million children who were murdered in the Holocaust; like the thousands upon thousands of children in Third World countries who die of malnutrition every year? Where will they reside — in an indeterminate limbo?

❖ ❖ ❖

Jewish tradition holds, reinforced by the *Kabbalah*, that concepts of heaven and hell are based on an underlying teaching that everyone has an immortal soul that must go somewhere after physical life ends. As quoted earlier, the *Kabbalah* "expounds on the theory of the mystics, that before releasing a soul for life on earth, the Creator splits it in two. The male part enters the male child and the female part enters the female child." Indeed, in the daily morning prayers, a Jews says:

> The soul that You have given me, O' God, is a pure one. You have created it and formed it, breathed it into me, and with me You sustain it.

If an immortal quality exists in a human being, does it depart from the body when the body dies? The typical views of heaven and hell have as their foundation the belief in the immortal soul that leaves the body at death. I would hope to gain support for this notion within the Bible, but, not only can I not find evidence of such a belief, the very recording of the creation of Adam, as mentioned before, seems to exclude the concept of an immortal soul:

> And the Lord God formed Adam of the dust of the ground, **and breathed into his nostrils the breath of life; and man became a living soul** (*Genesis* 2:7).

The soul did not give life to Adam. The breath of God gave life to Adam, and he was then a living soul. "Soul" is not used here in any profound way suggesting something separate and distinct from flesh or spirit. The key word modifying "soul" was "living." Adam was alive, so he was a soul. He would not have been a soul had he remained without the breath of life. He had to live, first, with breath. He had to be animated, living.

God told Adam and Eve, two "living souls," that they would "surely die" if they disobeyed the Divine Will (*Genesis* 2:17). God also told Adam that he was taken from the dust of the earth and he would return to dust (*Genesis* 3:19).

In the Old Testament, a human being is referred to as a "soul" (*nefesh* in Hebrew) more than one hundred and thirty times. The term is also applied to sea creatures, birds and land animals, including cattle and "creeping" creatures, such as reptiles and insects (*Genesis* 1:20-30).

If we make an argument for human beings possessing an immortal soul, animals must also have immortal souls, since the same Hebrew word is used for humans and animals alike. The truth is, the term "soul" refers to any living creature (whether human or beast), not to some separate, living essence temporarily inhabiting the body. Yet no biblical scholar would seriously make such a claim for animals.

Among the more explicit statements in the Bible about what happens to the soul at death are two found in *Ezekiel* 18:4 & 20. Both passages clearly state that "the soul who sins **shall die**." Not only do these scriptural passages show that the soul dies, but the soul is identified as a physical being, not a separate spirit having an existence independent of its physical host. This is given further credence in *Ecclesiastes*: "For the living know that they will die; but the dead know nothing..." (9:5). In short, the dead do not have consciousness.

So, whence the idea that the body goes to the grave at death and the soul continues to exist as a separate conscious entity? The *New Bible Dictionary* offers this background of the non-biblical nature of the immortal soul doctrine:

> The Greeks thought of the body as a hindrance to true life, and they looked for the time when the soul would be free from its shackles. They conceived of life after death in terms of the immortality of the soul...

Belief in a separate soul and body was popular in Greek society and was taught by one of Greece's most famous philosophers, Plato (427 B.C.E.-347 B.C.E.), who posited that the soul was self-moving and indivisible, existing before the body which it inhabited, ultimately surviving it.

How can I, a Jew, accept a Greek view of the world? The Greeks were basically pagans. I cannot, so I read:

> For You will not leave my soul in *Sheol*, nor will You allow Your Holy One to see corruption (*Psalms* 16:10).

This is a clear indication that after death we return to the dust from which we were fashioned, and see corruption; but our soul, as postulated in the *Kabbalah*, our soul, which never dies nor sleeps, having an immortal subsistence, immediately returns to God who provided it. And, perhaps, waits for another time to walk upon the earth.

> Lord, what are we that You have regard for us? What are we that You are mindful of us? We are like a breath; our days are as a

passing shadow; we come and go like grass, which in the morning shoots up, renewed, and in the evening fades and withers. You cause us to revert to dust, saying: "Return, O' mortal creatures!" Would that we were wise, that we understood where we are going. For when we die, we carry nothing away; our glory does not accompany us... **You redeem the soul of your servants, and none who trust in You shall be desolate** (*Psalms* 144:3-4, *Psalms* 90:6, *Deuteronomy* 32:29, *Psalms* 34:23).

Who knows? This is a reasonable thought — redeeming the soul of your servants; and it serves as perhaps the most compelling reason to believe in God. The way I look at it: If it is impossible to fathom the beginning, how can we comprehend the end? Why not hold out for some hope that something (anything), even as ill-defined as a soul, lingers on for eternity?

The End of the Beginning

I have completely exhausted myself, and, I am afraid that I have run out of time. What has driven me to struggle with my belief, and to question God, which obviously suggests that deep down I believe in the existence of some sort of Deity? I am beginning to think it is less about finding out why I am going to die prematurely than it is about making sense out of my life. I cannot accept that I lived in a Godless world, nor can I accept that my children and grandchildren will grow up in a Godless world.

At the wedding of one of my daughters, which I officiated, I quoted from a popular Israeli song: *The Children of the Winter of 1973*, which referred to the Yom Kippur War. My daughter's birth was the result of her parents' love and passion in the aftermath of that war. The refrain of the song:

> You promised a dove, an olive branch. You promised peace in our home, spring and renewal. You swore to fulfill that promise. You promised a dove.

I did not see that promise through to its end, but in the midst of the continued turmoil that surrounds Israel, I tried to create a sense of security and tranquility and peace within our family, and to pass on to my children the desire to work for peace in a wider setting. No longer can I protect them. I helped them, guided them and supported them, and hopefully that help, guidance and support will lead them to create a peaceful home. As it is written:

> Of him who loves his wife as himself, of her who honors her husband more than herself, and of them who rear their children in the path of righteousness, Scripture says: "In your home, peace will reign" (*Talmud Yevamot* 62b).

This is the essence of what is known in Judaism as "ethical wills." According to Jewish tradition, community leaders, parents and grandparents left to their posterity neither material goods nor valuables, but values. These wills dealt with principles, not property. For example, in his ethical will, the great Eastern European Yiddish writer, Sholom Aleichem (born Solomon Rabinowitz, 1859-1916), left to his children the example of his Jewish commitment: "Live together in peace, bear not hatred for each other, help one another in bad times and pity the poor." The humorist, Sam Levenson (1911-1980), in an ethical will to his grandchildren (and children everywhere), noted that his unpaid debts were his greatest assets. He wrote to his grandchildren:

> Everything I own, I owe. I leave you not everything I never had, but everything I had in my lifetime — a good family, respect for learning, compassion for my fellowman and some four letter words for all occasions, like: "Help, give, care, feel and love."

These are the values that I hope will be my legacy. For me, a world without God is a world without values, existence without moral anchor, survival without purpose, a universe without order; and ultimately, life without meaning.

> Humans beings do not live forever... We live less than the time it takes to blink an eye, if we measure our lives against eternity. So, it may be asked, what value is there to human life? There is so much pain in the world. What does it mean to have to suffer so much if our lives are nothing more than the blink of an eye? A blink of an eye in itself is nothing. But, the eye that blinks, *that* is

something. A span of life is nothing. But, the man who lives that span, *he* is something. He can fill that tiny span with meaning, so that its quality is immeasurable though its quantity may be insignificant. A man must fill his life with meaning — meaning is not automatically given to life. It is hard work to fill one's life with meaning. A life filled with meaning is worthy of rest (*The Chosen*, by Chaim Potok).

I like believing that God has set before us polar positions, "good and bad, a blessing and a curse, life and death" (*Deuteronomy*, 30:15,19), giving us the free choice to achieve the best. Indeed, I would like to think that I lived a life of goodness and blessing. Since, with all my questions, I have not succeeded in solving the mystery of life and death — which, if I were able to, would give **Divine meaning** to my life — I must accept that, like all of us, I live in the "gray areas" of life, between the good and the bad, between the blessing and the curse. Yet, I do believe that I have made reasoned and decent choices, and therefore have filled my life with **meaning**, which "is not automatically given to life."

Might it be enough (maybe egocentric) to believe that I created God, attaching to Him or Her the ethical standards and moral values that have given meaning not only to my life, but hopefully to the lives of those in my family, and to the lives of people I have touched throughout the years? I do not believe that my illness is a result of fate or Divine Will, but rather a matter of bad luck with genes. I truly believe I am dying before my time is up. But, while I eventually will succumb to a liver disorder, the physical diminution of my life has no bearing on its emotional or moral worth.

Through my questioning, I have come to learn that while death is the crisis of our life, it need not be our enemy:

For each one of us the moment comes when the great nurse, death, takes man, the child, by the hand and quietly says: "It is time to go home. Night is coming. It is your bedtime, child of earth. Come, you're tired. Lie down at last in the quiet nursery of nature and sleep. Sleep well. The day is gone. Stars shine in the canopy of eternity" (*Peace of Mind*, Rabbi Joshua Loth Liebman, 1907-1948).

The dust returns to the earth as it was, and the **spirit** returns to God Who gave it (*Ecclesiastes* 12:7).

Spirit can be best defined in Jewish terms as a Divine Spark implanted in all of us at birth, which is antithetical to the moment of death:

The Creator planted a Divine sweet spirit in us all, and made it a guide to all mortals" (*Apocrypha* 1:5 — non-canonical Jewish literature written during the Second Temple Period, 536 B.C.E. — 70 C.E.).

As one who knows how mortal he is, I regret that I will not be able to observe a little bit of what will happen immediately after my death, including being present at my funeral. I would hope that I would be delighted by the tributes. One of my greatest fears of dying is that, with the passage of time, I will be forgotten. It would be as if I never existed.

As my Divine questioning comes to an end, I am beginning to think that it does not matter if God exists or not; or, if I can prove God's existence or not. Indeed, God's existence is not dependent on me. But, given my theory of the creation of the world as being Divinely fashioned, from which all creation emanates, my life, short as it is, was dependent on and a result of that one single miraculous Divine act. Therefore, as an offshoot of the Creation, I surely must have inherited a Divine Spark.

I cannot do much with that Spark of Divinity now. Sadly, for me, it is a flame barely flickering in the wind. All of us part from this world with things left unsaid. I would have liked to have had a chance to say something of significance, something that might have had a positive influence on my children. But perhaps, some of my Divine Spark has entered them, adding to their own Divine Spark. Perhaps, if my children and grandchildren perpetuate my name, I, too, will be one in a chain of Firsts and Lasts, at least for a few generations. Perhaps, I will be granted a measure of immortality through remembrance. I would like that. Give me a few more years, and I hope to tell you if this "death wish" comes true.

Like Jacob, who, upon waking from his dream of the ladder reaching into the heavens, said: "God is in this place, and I knew it not" (*Genesis* 28:16), I too did not fully appreciate God's Divine presence throughout my life. But now, after my exhausting ordeal, I not only acknowledge God's existence, but also recognize that "God [was and] is in this place," and I know it.

❖ ❖ ❖

It is June 6, 10:00 A.M., exactly ten days after I slipped into my coma. Being told by the doctors that the end is imminent, my wife, my children and my grandchildren have crowded into my room — everyone I love, gathering around my bedside to bid a final farewell. Sensing that the fateful and inevitable hour has arrived, one of my daughters takes my hand in hers. If I have one last Divine question, it is in the form of a plea: "God, watch over my family. They were the greatest gift You gave me."

It's the perfect moment — high drama. I feel overwhelmed by an unrelenting fatigue. No longer do I have the emotional or physical energy to cling to life. I need to sleep, to close my eyes, and say goodbye... forever. Though trembling, I must accept the unavoidable reality of my death, and peacefully **begin a new phase in my existence**, letting the forces of nature take over and the warm embrace of God envelop me.

Though I walk through the valley of the shadow of death, I will fear no harm, for You are with me... Only goodness and steadfast love shall pursue me all the days of my life, and **I will dwell in the house of the Lord for many long years** (*Psalms* 23:4,6).

And so, I am left no alternative, but to end my story at the beginning.